CONTEMPORARY'S

EXERCISING YOUR ENGLISH

Language Skills for Developing Writers

BOOK I

Project Editors
Betsy Rubin
Pat Fiene

CB
CONTEMPORARY
BOOKS
CHICAGO

Published by Contemporary Books, Inc.
Two Prudential Plaza, Chicago, Illinois 60601-6790
Manufactured in the United States of America
International Standard Book Number: 0-8092-4081-5

Editorial Director
Caren Van Slyke

Editorial
Karin Evans
Larry Johnson
Janice Bryant
Cliff Wirt

Editorial Production Manager
Norma Fioretti

Production Editor
Jean Farley Brown

Production Assistant
Marina Micari

Cover Design
Lois Koehler

Typography
Impressions, Inc.
Madison, Wisconsin

CONTENTS

TO THE LEARNER v

Skills Inventory: GRAMMAR AND USAGE 1

SKILLS INVENTORY EVALUATION CHART 4

Answers and Explanations: SKILLS INVENTORY 5

SENTENCE EXERCISES
  1: Sentence Structure 7
  2: Fragments 8
  3: Commands and Questions 9
  4: Sentence Structure Review 10

NOUN EXERCISES
  5: Nouns 12
  6: Regular Plurals I 13
  7: Regular Plurals II 14
  8: Irregular Plurals 15
  9: Plurals Review 16
  10: Possessive Case I 17
  11: Possessive Case II 18
  12: Countable and Uncountable Nouns 19
  13: Noun Review 20

VERB EXERCISES
  14: Verbs 22
  15: Past Tense Regular Verbs 23
  16: Past Tense Irregular Verbs 24
  17: All Tenses I 25
  18: All Tenses II 27
  19: Verb Review 29

SUBJECT AND VERB AGREEMENT EXERCISES
  20: Subject and Verb Agreement 31
  21: Auxiliaries and *Being* Verbs 32
  22: Phrases and Gerunds 33
  23: Inverted Sentences 34
  24: Collective Nouns 35
  25: Indefinite Pronouns 36
  26: Compound Subjects I 37
  27: Compound Subjects II 38
  28: Relative Pronouns 39
  29: Agreement Review 40

PRONOUN EXERCISES

30: Pronouns 42

31: Compounds and Pronouns 43

32: *Who* and *Whom* 44

33: *To Be* and Comparisons..........................45

34: Appositives, Reflexives, Possessives 46

35: Number and Person I....................47

36: Number and Person II 48

37: Pronoun Review 49

ADJECTIVE AND ADVERB EXERCISES

38: Adjectives and Adverbs.................................51

39: Adverbs 52

40: Predicate Adjectives 53

41: Negative Adverbs 55

42: *This/That, These/Those, A/An* 56

43: Adjective/Adverb Comparisons I 57

44: Adjective/Adverb Comparisons II 58

45: Adjective/Adverb Review 60

Final Skills Inventory: **GRAMMAR AND USAGE**.............62

FINAL SKILLS INVENTORY EVALUATION CHART.......66

Answers and Explanations: **FINAL SKILLS INVENTORY**.....67

ANSWER KEY 69

TO THE LEARNER

Contemporary's *Exercising Your English: Book 1* is designed to help you develop a command of formal English grammar and usage. It is one of a series of three workbooks providing extensive practice in grammar, spelling, sentence structure, and other writing skills. Your instructor may assign the workbooks in one of several ways:

1) to supplement the grammar or writing reference book you are using in class
2) to use as main texts to reinforce in-class instruction
3) to use as self-study tools for help with the specific problems that appear in your writing.

Now here's a look at what you'll find in *Exercising Your English: Book 1.*

Skills Inventory

Your instructor may ask you to take the Skills Inventory test on pages 1–3 to pinpoint your own strengths and weaknesses in grammar. After you complete the Inventory, check your answers against the Answers and Explanations on pages 5–6. Then refer to the Skills Inventory Evaluation Chart on page 4 to see which exercises to emphasize as you work through this book.

Exercises

Before doing each exercise, read the brief grammar guide at the top of the page. This will help you focus on the grammar point you'll need to know to complete the exercise. Be sure, also, to read and follow the directions carefully as you do the exercise. Then check your answers by using the Answer Key in the back of this book. If you make more than a few errors, review the grammar guide, check your grammar reference book or perhaps a dictionary, or see your instructor for more help.

Extra Practice

Immediately following many exercises, you'll find Extra Practice exercises. These brief exercises give you the chance to apply the grammar or usage point to your own writing. Here you'll be able to say something about your own life or ideas. Since your answers will be your own—different from those of your classmates—no answers are provided in the back of the book.

Review Exercises

After each section is a review exercise that will help you pull together what you have just practiced. These exercises give you the chance to find out if you still need to study the area of grammar covered in the section. Be sure to check your answers against the Answer Key as soon as you complete the exercise.

Final Skills Inventory

When you have finished the workbook, you can take the Final Skills Inventory on pages 62–65 to see how well you have learned all the material you have practiced. Again, do be sure to check your answers against the Answers and Explanations that follow. If you discover you are still having problems, use the Final Skills Inventory Evaluation Chart on page 66 to identify the specific areas you need to review.

A Word About Grammar and Success

Exercising Your English: Book 1 gives you practice in formal, standard English grammar. Your mastery of this grammar will earn you respect and give you a head start for success in education and in the competitive job market. We hope you'll enjoy doing the exercises, and we wish you all the best in the future!

Skills Inventory   GRAMMAR AND USAGE

> **DIRECTIONS:** If one of the four underlined words or groups of words is an error in grammar or usage, blacken the space in the answer grid over the number corresponding to it. If there is no error, blacken the space numbered (5).

Example: In <u>most</u> <u>parts</u> of the country, winter <u>include</u> snow, ice, and freezing
$\quad$ 1 $\qquad$ 2 $\qquad\qquad$ 3

<u>temperatures</u>.
4

○ ○ ● ○ ○
1　2　3　4　5

1. <u>Students</u> often <u>respects</u> a teacher <u>who</u> is strict with <u>them</u>.
$\quad$ 1 $\qquad$ 2 $\qquad$ 3 $\qquad$ 4

1. ○ ○ ◎ ○ ○
$\quad$ 1　2　3　4　5

2. <u>This</u> <u>phenomena</u> is one of the <u>most</u> interesting I have <u>seen</u>.
$\quad$ 1 $\quad$ 2 $\qquad$ 3 $\qquad$ 4

2. ○ ○ ○ ○ ○
$\quad$ 1　2　3　4　5

3. <u>Neither</u> my boots <u>nor</u> my overcoat <u>are</u> <u>sufficiently</u> waterproof.
$\quad$ 1 $\qquad$ 2 $\qquad$ 3 $\quad$ 4

3. ○ ○ ○ ○ ○
$\quad$ 1　2　3　4　5

4. James <u>has</u> already <u>finish</u> <u>doing</u> the <u>hardest</u> crossword puzzle.
$\qquad$ 1 $\qquad$ 2 $\quad$ 3 $\qquad$ 4

4. ○ ○ ○ ○ ○
$\quad$ 1　2　3　4　5

5. The foods <u>us</u> Americans eat <u>are</u> different from <u>those</u> eaten in many
$\qquad$ 1 $\qquad$ 2 $\qquad$ 3

<u>other</u> countries.
4

5. ○ ○ ○ ○ ○
$\quad$ 1　2　3　4　5

6. Peanuts <u>is</u> a good, healthful <u>snack</u> because <u>they</u> <u>are</u> low in sugar.
$\qquad$ *are* /
$\qquad$ 1 $\qquad\qquad$ 2 $\qquad$ 3 $\quad$ 4

6. ○ ◐ ○ ○ ○
$\quad$ 1　2　3　4　5

7. Of <u>all</u> the musicals I have <u>seen</u>, I <u>enjoyed</u> *A Chorus Line* <u>more</u>.
$\quad$ 1 $\qquad$ 2 $\qquad$ 3 $\qquad$ 4

7. ○ ○ ○ ○ ○
$\quad$ 1　2　3　4　5

8. The <u>salespeople</u>—Mel, Marv, and Lon—<u>says</u> that sales are <u>lower</u> this
$\qquad$ 1 $\qquad\qquad$ 2 $\qquad$ 3

week <u>than</u> last.
$\qquad$ 4

8. ○ ○ ○ ○ ○
$\quad$ 1　2　3　4　5

9. Nobody <u>whom</u> <u>brings</u> a donation will <u>be</u> turned away <u>from</u> the
$\qquad$ 1 $\qquad$ 2 $\qquad$ 3 $\qquad$ 4

picnic.

9. ○ ○ ○ ○ ○
$\quad$ 1　2　3　4　5

10. <u>Who</u> <u>will</u> decide to <u>who</u> we report if <u>there</u> is an emergency?
$\quad$ 1 $\quad$ 2 $\qquad$ 3 $\qquad$ 4

10. ○ ○ ○ ○ ○
$\quad$ 1　2　3　4　5

11. Every dog in <u>Murphy's</u> kennel <u>barked</u> until <u>they</u> <u>received</u> more food.
$\qquad$ 1 $\qquad$ 2 $\qquad$ 3 $\quad$ 4

11. ○ ○ ○ ○ ○
$\quad$ 1　2　3　4　5

12. You <u>have</u> hardly <u>eaten</u> <u>none</u> of the food I <u>lovingly</u> prepared.
$\qquad$ 1 $\qquad$ 2 $\quad$ 3 $\qquad$ 4

12. ○ ○ ○ ○ ○
$\quad$ 1　2　3　4　5

13. <u>We</u> volunteers <u>worked</u> <u>long</u> and <u>patient</u> at our jobs.
$\quad$ 1 $\qquad$ 2 $\quad$ 3 $\qquad$ 4

13. ○ ○ ○ ○ ○
$\quad$ 1　2　3　4　5

14. Hamburger is <u>expensiver</u> <u>than</u> eggs <u>are</u>.
$\qquad$ 1 $\qquad$ 2 $\qquad$ 3 $\quad$ 4

14. ○ ○ ○ ○ ○
$\quad$ 1　2　3　4　5

15. <u>Your</u> <u>cheating</u> on the exam will not help you achieve <u>any</u> of <u>your</u>
$\quad$ 1 $\quad$ 2 $\qquad$ 3 $\quad$ 4

goals.

15. ○ ◐ ○ ○ ○
$\quad$ 1　2　3　4　5

(continued)

2

16. Between <u>you</u> and <u>I</u>, today is the <u>happiest</u> day of <u>my</u> life.
            1   2   3   4
    16. ○ ○ ○ ○ ○
        1 2 3 4 5

17. <u>Both</u> of the movies at the theater <u>were</u> <u>ran</u> last week <u>too</u>.
   1
    17. ○ ○ ○ ○ ○
        1 2 3 4 5

18. The other customers <u>whom</u> we met <u>were</u> even <u>angrier</u> than <u>we</u>.
    18. ○ ○ ○ ○ ○
        1 2 3 4 5

19. The man <u>who</u> <u>works</u> with <u>me</u> always talks to <u>hisself</u>.
    19. ○ ○ ○ ○ ○
        1 2 3 4 5

20. <u>Have</u> <u>you</u> <u>brung</u> <u>your</u> check to be cashed?
    20. ○ ○ ○ ○ ○
        1 2 3 4 5

21. Rae was <u>real</u> <u>upset</u> <u>when</u> the stain wouldn't come <u>out</u> of her dress.
    21. ○ ○ ○ ○ ○
        1 2 3 4 5

22. Statistics <u>show</u> that <u>much</u> women <u>work</u> at full-time jobs out of their
homes <u>as well as</u> raise families.
    22. ○ ○ ○ ○ ○
        1 2 3 4 5

23. Eva Peron never <u>become</u> vice-president of Argentina, <u>although</u> she
<u>wanted</u> the position <u>badly</u>.
    23. ○ ○ ○ ○ ○
        1 2 3 4 5

24. A car <u>with</u> front-wheel drive <u>handles</u> <u>well</u> on ice and snow; it parks
<u>easy</u>, too.
    24. ○ ○ ○ ○ ○
        1 2 3 4 5

25. The <u>telephone</u> <u>ringing</u> <u>woke</u> me from a <u>sound</u> sleep.
    25. ○ ○ ○ ○ ○
        1 2 3 4 5

26. The supervisor told <u>us</u> <u>we</u> must do our work more <u>careful</u> or we will
be <u>fired</u>.
    26. ○ ○ ○ ○ ○
        1 2 3 4 5

27. He is the man <u>whom</u> I <u>truly</u> <u>hope</u> <u>will win</u> the next election.
    27. ○ ○ ○ ○ ○
        1 2 3 4 5

28. Each of the team members <u>deserves</u> a medal because of <u>their</u> valiant
<u>efforts</u> in the <u>game's</u> final minutes.
    28. ○ ○ ○ ○ ○
        1 2 3 4 5

29. <u>Which</u> <u>is</u> <u>healthiest</u>, plain yogurt <u>or</u> cottage cheese?
    29. ○ ○ ○ ○ ○
        1 2 3 4 5

30. Michael, <u>who</u> is my nephew, <u>and</u> <u>his</u> fiancée, Carla, <u>make</u> a
wonderful couple.
    30. ○ ○ ○ ○ ○
        1 2 3 4 5

31. If Debbie felt <u>so</u> <u>weakly</u>, why <u>didn't</u> <u>she</u> stay home?
    31. ○ ○ ○ ○ ○
        1 2 3 4 5

32. In the future <u>there</u> <u>will</u> <u>be</u> <u>much</u> opportunities to use my computer.
    32. ○ ○ ○ ○ ○
        1 2 3 4 5

33. <u>A</u> urgent message was <u>left</u> on my desk, but <u>no one</u> had <u>signed</u> it.
    33. ○ ○ ○ ○ ○
        1 2 3 4 5

34. Jerry <u>hurted</u> his back <u>badly</u> while <u>carrying</u> the <u>heavy</u> boxes.
    <u>1</u>   <u>2</u>   <u>3</u>   <u>4</u>
    34. ◯ ◯ ◯ ◯ ◯
         1   2   3   4   5

35. These shoes are <u>more tight</u> than the <u>ones</u> I <u>usually</u> wear.
    <u>1</u>   <u>2</u>   <u>3</u>   <u>4</u>
    35. ◯ ◯ ◯ ◯ ◯
         1   2   3   4   5

36. <u>Whom</u> <u>is</u> <u>prettier</u>, Sharon or <u>I</u>?
    <u>1</u> <u>2</u> <u>3</u>   <u>4</u>
    36. ◯ ◯ ◯ ◯ ◯
         1   2   3   4   5

37. Nobody can <u>run</u> the relay race <u>faster</u> than <u>you</u> and <u>I</u>.
    <u>1</u>   <u>2</u>   <u>3</u>   <u>4</u>
    37. ◯ ◯ ◯ ◯ ◯
         1   2   3   4   5

38. Paula <u>doesn't</u> need <u>no</u> doctor to tell <u>her</u> to quit smoking while she <u>is</u>
    <u>1</u>   <u>2</u>   <u>3</u>   <u>4</u>
    pregnant.
    38. ◯ ◯ ◯ ◯ ◯
         1   2   3   4   5

39. All of <u>those</u> <u>radioes</u> are too <u>expensive</u> for <u>us</u> to consider.
    <u>1</u>   <u>2</u>   <u>3</u>   <u>4</u>
    39. ◯ ◯ ◯ ◯ ◯
         1   2   3   4   5

40. Many <u>people</u> wish <u>they</u> could forget <u>their</u> <u>pasts</u>.
    <u>1</u>   <u>2</u>   <u>3</u> <u>4</u>
    40. ◯ ◯ ◯ ◯ ◯
         1   2   3   4   5

41. File your tax forms <u>prompt</u> in order to <u>get</u> <u>your</u> refund <u>early</u>.
    <u>1</u>   <u>2</u> <u>3</u>   <u>4</u>
    41. ◯ ◯ ◯ ◯ ◯
         1   2   3   4   5

42. Some of the <u>tools</u> in the <u>cabinet</u> <u>is</u> in need of <u>cleaning</u> and oiling.
    <u>1</u>   <u>2</u> <u>3</u>   <u>4</u>
    42. ◯ ◯ ◯ ◯ ◯
         1   2   3   4   5

43. Every <u>one</u> of the <u>students</u> <u>has</u> three <u>mouses</u> in his experiment.
    <u>1</u>   <u>2</u>   <u>3</u>   <u>4</u>
    43. ◯ ◯ ◯ ◯ ◯
         1   2   3   4   5

44. Cross country <u>skiing</u> and ice skating <u>is</u> <u>popular</u> winter <u>sports</u>.
    <u>1</u>   <u>2</u> <u>3</u>   <u>4</u>
    44. ◯ ◯ ◯ ◯ ◯
         1   2   3   4   5

45. Will <u>you</u> remind <u>everyone</u> to <u>bring</u> <u>their</u> donations for the food
    <u>1</u>   <u>2</u>   <u>3</u> <u>4</u>
    drive?
    45. ◯ ◯ ◯ ◯ ◯
         1   2   3   4   5

46. The new <u>employees</u> always <u>feel</u> <u>many</u> anxiety about <u>their</u>
    <u>1</u>   <u>2</u> <u>3</u>   <u>4</u>
    performance on the job.
    46. ◯ ◯ ◯ ◯ ◯
         1   2   3   4   5

47. <u>Childrens'</u> <u>pajamas</u> must be fireproof, <u>although</u> <u>adults'</u> do not have to
    <u>1</u>   <u>2</u>   <u>3</u>   <u>4</u>
    be.
    47. ◯ ◯ ◯ ◯ ◯
         1   2   3   4   5

48. The town looked <u>strangely</u> all <u>covered</u> with <u>deep</u> <u>white</u> snow.
    <u>1</u>   <u>2</u>   <u>3</u> <u>4</u>
    48. ◯ ◯ ◯ ◯ ◯
         1   2   3   4   5

49. Gloria takes <u>her</u> aerobic <u>dance</u> routines <u>seriouser</u> than <u>I</u> take my
    <u>1</u>   <u>2</u>   <u>3</u>   <u>4</u>
    bookkeeping.
    49. ◯ ◯ ◯ ◯ ◯
         1   2   3   4   5

50. Blake is one of those people <u>who</u> always <u>work</u> <u>harder</u> than <u>anyone</u>
    <u>1</u>   <u>2</u>   <u>3</u>   <u>4</u>
    else.
    50. ◯ ◯ ◯ ◯ ◯
         1   2   3   4   5

SKILLS INVENTORY EVALUATION CHART

DIRECTIONS: After completing the Skills Inventory, check your answers by using the Skills Inventory Answers and Explanations, pages 5–6. Write the total number of your *correct* answers for each skill area in the blank boxes below. If you have *one or more incorrect* answers in any skill area, you need more practice. Exercises to study in this workbook are listed in the Exercise Numbers column.

Skill Area	Item Number	Total	Number Correct	Exercise Numbers
Plural Nouns	2, 39, 43	3	____	6–9
Possessive Nouns	25, 47	2	____	10–11
Countable and Uncountable Nouns	22, 32, 46	3	____	12
Verb Tenses	4, 17, 20, 23, 34	5	____	15–18
Subject-Verb Agreement	1, 3, 6, 8, 42, 44	6	____	20–28
Pronoun Case	5, 9, 10, 16, 19, 27, 36	7	____	30–34
Pronoun Number and Person	11, 28, 45	3	____	35–36
Adjective Form	31, 33, 48	3	____	38, 40, 42
Adverb Form	13, 21, 24, 41	4	____	38–41
Negative Adverbs	12, 38	2	____	41
Adjective Comparison	14, 29, 35	3	____	43–44
Adverb Comparison	7, 26, 49	3	____	43–44
(NO ERROR: Items 15, 18, 30, 37, 40, 50)				

Note: A score of 32 or more correct is considered passing for this Inventory.

Answers and Explanations   SKILLS INVENTORY

> **DIRECTIONS:** After completing the Skills Inventory (pages 1–3), use the Answers and Explanations to check your work. *On these pages,* circle the number of each item you correctly answered. Then turn to the Skills Inventory Evaluation Chart (page 4) and follow the directions given.

1. **(2)** The verb *respect* is needed because the subject *students* is plural.

2. **(2)** The singular noun *phenomenon* is needed because of the singular demonstrative pronoun *this*.

3. **(3)** When a compound subject is joined by *neither . . . nor,* the verb agrees with the subject nearer to the verb. *Overcoat* is singular, so the correct verb is *is.*

4. **(2)** The correct past participle is *finished.*

5. **(1)** The subjective pronoun *we* is needed to go with the verb *eat.*

6. **(1)** The verb *are* is needed because the subject *peanuts* is plural.

7. **(4)** *Most* is needed to show a comparison of more than two things.

8. **(2)** The verb *say* is needed because the subject *salespeople* is plural.

9. **(1)** The subjective pronoun *who* is needed to go with the verb *brings.*

10. **(3)** The objective pronoun *whom* is needed because it comes after a preposition *(to).*

11. **(3)** The singular pronoun *it* is needed because it refers to the singular subject *Every dog.*

12. **(3)** The positive *any* is needed because the sentence already contains a negative, *hardly.*

13. **(4)** The adverb *patiently* is needed to tell how we worked.

14. **(2)** The correct comparative adjective form is *more expensive.*

15. **(5)** No error

16. **(2)** The objective pronoun *me* is needed because it comes after a preposition *(between).*

17. **(3)** The correct past participle form of the verb is *run.*

18. **(5)** No error

19. **(4)** The correct reflexive pronoun form is *himself.*

20. **(3)** The correct past participle form is *brought.*

21. **(1)** The adverb *really* is needed to modify the adjective *upset.*

22. **(2)** The adjective *many* is needed because *women* is a countable noun.

23. **(1)** The correct past form is *became.*

24. **(4)** The adverb *easily* is needed to modify the verb *parks.*

(continued)

6

25. (1) The possessive form *telephone's* is needed before the gerund *ringing*.

26. (3) The adverb form *carefully* is needed to tell how we must do our work.

27. (1) The subjective pronoun *who* is needed to go with the verb *will win*.

28. (2) The singular pronoun *his (or her)* is needed because it refers to *each*, which is singular.

29. (3) The comparative form of the adjective *healthier* is needed because two things are being compared.

30. (5) No error

31. (2) The adjective form *weak* is needed after the nonaction verb *felt*.

32. (4) The adjective *many* or an expression such as *a lot of* is needed because *opportunities* is a countable noun.

33. (1) *An* is needed because *urgent* begins with a vowel sound.

34. (1) The correct past form is *hurt*.

35. (2) The correct comparative form is *tighter*.

36. (1) The subjective pronoun *Who* is needed to go with the verb *is*.

37. (5) No error

38. (2) *A* or *any* is needed because the sentence already has a negative, *doesn't*.

39. (2) The correct plural of *radio* is *radios*.

40. (5) No error

41. (1) The adverb form *promptly* is needed to tell how to file.

42. (3) The verb *are* is needed because the subject *some* is plural in this sentence.

43. (4) The correct plural of *mouse* is *mice*.

44. (2) The verb *are* is needed to go with the plural compound subjects *skiing* and *ice skating*.

45. (4) The singular pronouns *his or her* are needed to refer to *everyone*, which is singular.

46. (3) The adjective *much* or an expression such as *a great deal of* is needed because *anxiety* is an uncountable noun.

47. (1) The correct possessive form of *children* is *children's*.

48. (1) The adjective form *strange* is needed. It is a predicate adjective describing the town.

49. (3) The correct comparative adverb form is *more seriously*.

50. (5) No error

Complete the Skills Inventory Evaluation Chart on page 4.

Exercise 1   SENTENCE STRUCTURE

A **sentence** consists of a **subject** and a **predicate** that communicate a complete thought. The part of a sentence that tells who or what the sentence is about is called the **simple subject.** The **simple predicate** (or simple verb) tells what the subject does or is. Both parts of a sentence can have other words added to give more information about the simple subject and the simple predicate:

Fred and Gloria are planning a trip downtown next weekend.
   Simple Subject = *Fred and Gloria* (who)
   Simple Predicate = *are planning* (what the subject is doing)

DIRECTIONS: In each of the following sentences, underline the simple subject once and the simple predicate twice.

Example: After Father's Day those <u>ties</u> <u>will be sold</u> for half price.

1. My <u>dentist</u> <u>works</u> very slowly and carefully.
2. The weight-lifters practiced their breathing.
3. The <u>truck drivers</u> <u>have been</u> on strike for two days.
4. The <u>day-care</u> center <u>opens</u> at 8:00 a.m.
5. Gloria's widowed <u>mother</u> <u>is moving</u> in with her.
6. My <u>partner</u> <u>will deliver</u> the flowers at noon.
7. The new suntan creams prevent burning.
8. <u>David</u> <u>left</u> school after 10th grade.
9. Instead of macaroni, the <u>chef</u> <u>prepared</u> lasagna.
10. The article in the *Tribune* <u>moved</u> me to tears.

EXTRA PRACTICE

Complete the following sentences by adding a simple subject or a simple predicate of your choice.

1. _Lifetime_ is a good TV show. (Add a subject)
2. I _like_ detective shows. (Add a predicate)
3. My favorite _____ is pizza. (Add a subject)
4. In my opinion, _France/Swizland_ is the perfect place to go on vacation. (Add a subject)
5. I _am_ speaking in front of groups of people. (Add a predicate)

Answers begin on page 69.

8

Exercise 2 FRAGMENTS

An incomplete sentence is called a **sentence fragment.** A fragment may lack either a subject or a predicate. It may also be incomplete because it does not communicate a complete thought. To test your sentences to see if they are complete, ask and answer the following questions:

    1) Does the sentence have a subject?
    2) Does the sentence have a predicate?
    3) Does the sentence express a complete thought?

If you can answer "yes" to these three questions, the sentence is complete.

DIRECTIONS: Use the three questions above to decide whether each group of words is a sentence or a fragment. Mark "S" for sentence or "F" for fragment in the blank at the right.

Example: Got ink all over my hands.   _____ *F*

1. He chews only sugarless gum.   1. ___ S
2. Puts her briefcase on her desk.   2. ___ F
3. Everyone who came to the lecture.   3. ___ F
4. Am looking for a road map of Texas.   4. ___ F
5. The atlas is no help.   5. ___ S
6. Air-conditioning uses a great deal of energy.   6. ___ S
7. As the papers blew all over the room.   7. ___ F
8. The minimum wage for part-time workers.   8. ___ F
9. The gun control bill is not popular with this group.   9. ___ S
10. Seeing the price of gold double within a week.   10. ___ F
11. Just because he has a high school diploma.   11. ___ F
12. The noise startled everyone.   12. ___ S
13. Drugs, cause of so much concern in the 1990s.   13. ___ F
14. The quartz watch runs on a tiny battery.   14. ___ S
15. Taking care not to waste any time.   15. ___ F
16. Only had instant coffee or tea.   16. ___ F
17. Larry has taken the test four times now.   17. ___ S
18. Without any improvement in his scores.   18. ___ F
19. We must end the dumping of toxic waste!   19. ___ S
20. Officials elected by the people in the district.   20. ___ F

Answers begin on page 69.

Exercise 3   COMMANDS AND QUESTIONS

Two types of sentences are more difficult to test for completeness.
1) The **command:** *Bring me some pie and coffee.*
   The simple subject *you* is not written or spoken; instead, it is said to be "understood."
2) The **question:** *Has the cook made the soup for today?*
   The simple subject *cook* separates *has* and *made,* the two parts of the simple predicate.

> **DIRECTIONS:** In each of the following sentences, underline the simple subject once and the simple predicate twice. If a subject is understood, write it in parentheses after the sentence.

Example: Open *the door. (you).*

1. Leave me alone. *You*
2. Have you met the new tenants?
3. When will the alarm ring?
4. Where is the spare tire?
5. Climb down the fire escape. *You*
6. Why did Alex quit his job?
7. Please bring me a bucket and a mop.
8. Can anyone read the instructions on this package?
9. Abandon ship! *(You)*
10. How could the floor be so sticky?
11. Turn down that radio! *You*
12. What is the solution to the problem?
13. Did you enjoy the party?
14. Are the hamburgers ready?
15. Wash the dishes. *(You)*

EXTRA PRACTICE

Write six sentences as follows:

three **commands** that you might say to a family member

three **questions** that your instructor might ask you

(handwritten answers)
1 Clean the kitchen
2 Don't make me good night.
3. Bought some apple and banana.

* Has everyone copy the note in your book?
* Can you read this page ?. me
* Could you please earse the blackboard?

Answers begin on page 69.

Exercise 4   SENTENCE STRUCTURE REVIEW

> **DIRECTIONS:** If there is a sentence fragment in the following groups, blacken the space in the answer grid over the number corresponding to it. If all of the choices are complete sentences, blacken the space numbered (5).

Example:

   (1) All the washing machines are being used.
   (2) Do you need some help?
   (3) And down the street.
   (4) He is such a bother!

   ○ ○ ● ○ ○
   1 2 3 4 5

1. (1) The flowers bloomed early.
   (2) Will you look at that?
   (3) Larry has lost his car keys again.
   (4) Used hair spray instead of deodorant.

   1. ○ ○ ○ ◉ ○
      1 2 3 4 5

2. (1) Never studied when they were in school.
   (2) Your tie is wild!
   (3) Richard lost nearly twenty pounds.
   (4) Whole wheat flour is brown.

   2. ◉ ○ ○ ○ ○
      1 2 3 4 5

3. (1) The apartment has been rented.
   (2) Here are some messages for you.
   (3) Maria's English is improving.
   (4) Jessica Lange is a fine actress.

   3. ○ ◉ ○ ○ ○
      1 2 3 4 5

4. (1) We ate in the non-smoking section.
   (2) Wasn't an empty seat on the flight.
   (3) Clouds gathered before the storm.
   (4) That is just too expensive!

   4. ○ ◉ ○ ○ ○
      1 2 3 4 5

5. (1) An early morning walk along the lake.
   (2) Who eloped?
   (3) Can someone translate this?
   (4) Maury and Gisella are Greek.

   5. ○ ○ ◉ ○ ○
      1 2 3 4 5

6. (1) The basic training camp is in Louisiana.
   (2) The garage roof is leaking.
   (3) Took a hot shower and felt better.
   (4) Those false nails look like claws!

   6. ○ ○ ◉ ○ ○
      1 2 3 4 5

7. (1) Jan always clips newspaper coupons.
   (2) His children are living with his ex-wife.
   (3) The fire caused smoke damage.
   (4) Taco shells should be crisp, not soggy.

   7. ○ ○ ○ ○ ○
      1 2 3 4 5

8. (1) People who buy on credit.
   (2) I love Italian opera.
   (3) Isn't Eddie Murphy something?
   (4) The new highway will open next week.

8. ○ ○ ◉ ○ ○
   1 2 3 4 5

9. (1) Stephanie Mills is fantastic!
   (2) After one year of work, you will have one week's vacation.
   (3) During the entire race for the gold medal.
   (4) Anyone who can operate a computer will be hired.

9. ○ ○ ◉ ○ ○
   1 2 3 4 5

10. (1) The programs on public television are educational.
    (2) The new Hispanic members of the school board.
    (3) Our furnace broke down.
    (4) The movers relaxed with cold beers.

10. ○ ◉ ○ ○ ○
    1 2 3 4 5

11. (1) That was a close call!
    (2) Wash your hands.
    (3) Could have been a real expert.
    (4) Call me after dinner, please.

11. ○ ○ ○ ○ ○
    1 2 3 4 5

12. (1) Are you sure?
    (2) Have you got a flashlight?
    (3) We won!
    (4) Where was the accident?

12. ○ ○ ○ ○ ○
    1 2 3 4 5

13. (1) Lives in a dangerous time and place.
    (2) The beaches are closed.
    (3) There are many reasons for the policy.
    (4) I enjoy chocolate in any form.

13. ○ ○ ○ ○ ○
    1 2 3 4 5

14. (1) The fans were thrilled.
    (2) Who will take their children?
    (3) Which type of heat does your building have?
    (4) From a tanker in the lake.

14. ○ ○ ○ ○ ○
    1 2 3 4 5

15. (1) It is from a myth.
    (2) Even when I diet, I eat some chocolate.
    (3) Is that very American?
    (4) Look at all the crime reports!

15. ○ ○ ○ ◉ ○
    1 2 3 4 5

16 (1) Leave!
   (2) The best dancer of all.
   (3) Who called?
   (4) Here is the report.

16. ◉ ○ ○ ○ ○
    1 2 3 4 5

17. (1) Eat more vegetables.
    (2) That is interesting.
    (3) To lose weight and feel better.
    (4) We left.

17. ○ ○ ○ ○ ○
    1 2 3 4 5

18. (1) Did we win?
    (2) I don't know.
    (3) There is your answer.
    (4) Look out!

18. ○ ○ ○ ◉ ○
    1 2 3 4 5

Answers begin on page 69.

12

Exercise 5   NOUNS

A **noun** is a word that names a person, place, thing, or idea:

Melinda chose a new *backpack* from the *samples*.

DIRECTIONS: In each of the following sentences, four words have been underlined. If one of the four words is a noun, blacken the space in the answer grid over the number corresponding to it. If none of the four words is a noun, blacken the space over number (5).

Example: John Bass has his own company.
  1   2   3   4

● ○ ○ ○ ○
1 2 3 4 5

1. The bus stopped at the corner near the new shopping
   1   2   3   4
   center.

1. ○ ○ ○ ○ ○
   1 2 3 4 5

2. When a husband and wife both work, they often share
   1   2   3   4
   chores at home.

2. ○ ○ ○ ○ ○
   1 2 3 4 5

3. If the bus drivers decide to go on strike, I will have to
   1
   get to my job another way.
   2   3   4

3. ○ ○ ○ ○ ○
   1 2 3 4 5

4. Today's newspaper predicts higher taxes in the future
   1   2
   instead of lower ones.
   3   4

4. ○ ○ ○ ○ ○
   1 2 3 4 5

5. The pictures from Nancy's thirty-fifth birthday party were
   1   2   3
   wonderful.
   4

5. ○ ○ ○ ○ ○
   1 2 3 4 5

6. Evelyn is starting another new diet, but we know she
   1   2   3   4
   won't stay on it.

6. ○ ○ ○ ○ ○
   1 2 3 4 5

7. Some high schools offer classes that teach students how
   1   2   3
   to practice self-defense.
   4

7. ○ ○ ○ ○ ○
   1 2 3 4 5

8. I wonder if it is wise to marry young; maybe we would
   1   2   3
   have fewer divorces if people waited longer to marry.
   4

8. ○ ○ ○ ○ ○
   1 2 3 4 5

EXTRA PRACTICE

Make a list of ten nouns. Include in your list persons, places, things, and ideas.

Answers begin on page 69.

Exercise 6   REGULAR PLURALS I

A **plural** noun names *more than one* person, place, thing, or idea:

Many *families* buy *homes* to save money on *taxes*.

There are rules for forming the plurals of nouns. Here are the three most basic rules:
1) The plural of most nouns is formed by adding *s:*
    car, cars; sale, sales; desk, desks
2) The plural of nouns ending with *s, sh, ch, x,* or *z* is formed by adding *es:*
    brush, brushes; box, boxes
3) The plural of nouns that end with *y* after a consonant is formed by changing *y* to *i* and adding *es:*
    baby, babies; city, cities

Note: The plural of nouns that end with *y* after a vowel is formed by adding *s:*
    day, days; attorney, attorneys

DIRECTIONS: If there is an incorrect plural form in the group of nouns, circle it. Then write the correct spelling on the line. If all of the plurals are correct, write "OK" on the line.

Example: ducks wishes catches (crashs) ___crashes___

1. eagles thrushes parrots finches _____
2. delays pennys keys stories _____
3. watches bracelets necklaces crownes _____
4. buggies candies bluejays blueberrys _____
5. riches hopes kisses witchs _____
6. turkeys studies puppys cavities _____
7. blazes dashes blotches blanketes _____
8. secretarys directories mysteries volleys _____

EXTRA PRACTICE

A mother and child are taking a bus trip. They have packed two each of the items below. Write a paragraph describing the bus trip. In your paragraph, use the correct **plural form** of these items:

sweater

dress

lunch

toothbrush

toy

battery

Answers begin on page 69.

Exercise 7   REGULAR PLURALS II

Here are more rules for forming the plurals of nouns.

4) The plural of nouns ending with *f* or *fe* is sometimes formed by adding *s;* sometimes it is formed by changing the *f* or *fe* to *v* and adding *es:*

   roof, roofs; thief, thieves; knife, knives

5) The plural of most nouns ending in *o* is formed by adding *s*. Sometimes the same words can end in *s* or *es;* check your dictionary if you are not sure. The following words *always* end in *es:*

   tomato, tomatoes; potato, potatoes; echo, echoes; hero, heroes; torpedo, torpedoes

6) The plural of hyphenated nouns is formed by adding *s* to the main noun:

   father-in-law, fathers-in-law; vice-president, vice-presidents

7) The plural of nouns ending with *ful* is formed by adding *s* to the end of the word:

   spoonful, spoonfuls

DIRECTIONS: If there is an incorrect plural form in the group of nouns, circle it. Then write the correct spelling on the line. If all of the plurals are correct, write "OK" on the line.

Example:	*videos*	(*pianoes*)	*solos*	*heroes*	*pianos*
1. tomatos	potatoes	tornados	toes		
2. sisters-in-law	half-brothers	attorneys-at-laws	masters-of-ceremonies		
3. mouthfuls	bagsful	handfuls	drawerfuls		
4. cousins-to-be	mothers-in-law	great-aunts	brother-in-laws		
5. echoes	shelves	autos	wives		
6. lives	bookshelves	knifes	beliefs		
7. altos	stereos	photoes	radios		
8. leafs	proofs	halves	calves		
9. banjos	burros	cellos	sopranos		
10. mosquitoes	hoboes	videos	potatos		
11. briefs	puffs	tariffs	safes		
12. cupsful	armfuls	bowlfuls	boxfuls		
13. memos	cameos	studioes	duos		
14. lookers-on	runners-up	brides-to-be	senator-elects		

Answers begin on page 69.

Exercise 8   IRREGULAR PLURALS

Below are examples of plural nouns with different types of irregular spellings.

8) For some nouns, the plural form is the same as the singular form:

> one fish, two fish; one deer, two deer

9) Some nouns can be used only in the plural form:

> binoculars; scissors

10) The plural of some nouns is formed by changing the spelling:

> tooth, teeth; mouse, mice; child, children; person, people

11) The plural of nouns ending with man, woman, or child is formed by using the plural forms men, women, or children:

> salesman, salesmen; superwoman, superwomen

12) The plural of some nouns ending in is is formed by changing is to es:

> crisis, crises; basis, bases; hypothesis, hypotheses

13) The plural of some nouns ending in um or on is formed by changing the um or on to a:

> datum, data; memorandum, memoranda; criterion, criteria; phenomenon, phenomena

> **DIRECTIONS:** If there is an incorrect plural form in the group of nouns, circle it. Then write the correct spelling on the line. If all of the plurals are correct, write "OK" on the line.

Example:	teeth	scissors	(memorandes)	parentheses	*memoranda*
1. mice	trout	fish	sheep	
2. children	repairmen	crisies	hypotheses	
3. sunglass	trousers	shorts	jeans	
4. policemans	bases	feet	washerwomen	
5. cattle	pants	data	tooths	
6. clothes	slacks	overalls	briefs	
7. servicewomans	lice	eyeglasses	moose	
8. swordfish	deers	cows	horses	
9. godchilds	godparents	chairwomen	chairmen	
10. analyses	criterias	memoranda	media	

Exercise 9   PLURALS REVIEW

DIRECTIONS: Write the plural form of each noun.

Example: *handful*   *handfuls*

1. city — *cities*
2. church — *churchs*
3. chairwoman — *chairwomen*
4. crisis — *crisises*
5. monkey — *monkeies*
6. brother-in-law — *babies* *brothers-in*
7. baby — *babies*
8. tooth — *teeth*
9. belief — *beliefs*
10. solo — *solos*
11. check — *checks*
12. potato — *potatos*
13. wife — *wifes*
14. story — *stories*
15. light — *lights*
16. replay — *replays*
17. spoonful — *spoonfuls*
18. fish — *fishs*
19. bookshelf — *bookshelves*
20. grandchild — *grandchildren*
21. vacancy — *vacancies*
22. crash — *crashes*
23. annex — *annexes*
24. quartz — *quartzes*
25. criterion — *criterions*

Answers begin on page 69.

Exercise 10   POSSESSIVE CASE I

The **possessive** form of a noun shows ownership or relationship:

Peter's jacket is down-filled.

Here are the rules for forming the possessive of regular nouns:
1) The possessive of singular nouns is formed by adding *'s*. Even when a singular noun ends in *s*, add *'s* to form the possessive:

   Mr. *Liss's* car; the *girl's* address

2) The possessive of plural nouns ending with an *s* is formed by adding only the apostrophe:

   four *hours'* sleep; the *Perezes'* new home

DIRECTIONS: Each underlined noun in the following sentences has been made possessive. If the underlined word is not correctly used or spelled, write the corrected word on the blank. If it is correct, write "OK."

Example: *My sisters' wallet was stolen.*   _____sister's_____

1. Did John's mother call this morning?   _____ok_____
2. This bus' windows are all steamed up.   _____
3. My landlords rules are ridiculous; he is so unreasonable.   _____
4. All of the miner's wives waited for their safe return.   _____
5. Steve is taking two week's vacation.   _____
6. Have you had that cat's claws removed?   _____
7. Those protester's complaints never reached the mayor.   _____
8. Dr. Jones' office is in the new medical center.   _____
9. Most parent's choice seems to be to keep the schools open.   _____
10. Three companies' licenses were revoked.   _____
11. Have city worker's jobs been cut?   _____
12. Mr. Gross' family all respect him.   _____
13. The restaurant launders its waitresses' uniforms free of charge.   _____
14. What is todays' date?   _____
15. Boy's shoes are now on sale.   _____

EXTRA PRACTICE

Write a sentence for each of the following possessive nouns:

the singular possessive of *company*

the plural possessive of *company*

the plural possessive of *church*

Answers begin on page 70.

Exercise 11   POSSESSIVE CASE II

Two types of noun possessives require extra attention: plural nouns with irregular spellings and nouns that precede gerunds.

3) To form the possessive of plural nouns that do *not* end in *s,* add *'s:*

   men's locker room; *children's* department

4) **Gerunds** are nouns that end in *ing.* Nouns that *precede* gerunds must be possessive to show the relationship between the two words:

   The *family's arguing* has gotten worse.

   Ed's writing has really improved!

DIRECTIONS: If there is an error in a sentence, correct the error on the line provided. If a sentence is correct, write "OK" on the line.

Example: *Judi cracking her gum annoys me.*

   Judi's cracking her gum annoys me.

1. José repairing his car made a lot of noise.

   _____

2. David driving made me nervous.

   _____

3. Did the children's mother just leave them?

   _____

4. Who is the peoples' choice for mayor?

   _____

5. His father's drinking greatly disturbed him.

   _____

6. Molly Yard fights for womens' rights.

   _____

7. Steve cooking is a joke.

   _____

8. The men's softball team challenged the women's team.

   _____

9. We worry about Sally drinking alcohol.

   _____

10. Many people's property was damaged.

   _____

Answers begin on page 70.

Exercise 12   COUNTABLE AND UNCOUNTABLE NOUNS

Countable nouns refer to persons, places, things, or ideas that can be enumerated, or counted, such as *one idea, two ideas* or *one machine, two machines.*

As these examples show, countable nouns have singular and plural forms. **Uncountable** nouns cannot be counted and do not have plural forms. For example, there is no such thing as *two knowledges* or *ten equipments.*

1) Some words can be used only with plural countable nouns:

   many people, *a number of* reasons, *few* students, *fewer* teachers, *these* books, *those* bananas

2) Some words can be used only with uncountable nouns:

   much happiness, *a great deal of* work, *little* luck, *less* money

Some words can be used with both singular and uncountable nouns:

   this, that

DIRECTIONS: Correct the underlined part of the following sentences. Write the corrected sentence in the space. If there is no error in the sentence, write "OK."

Example: I have too <u>much</u> assignments to do.
   I have too many assignments to do.

1. Potatoes have <u>less</u> calories than you might think.

   _____

2. <u>This</u> suggestions are very helpful.

   _____

3. How <u>many</u> problems can one family have?

   _____

4. The boss assigned <u>fewer</u> work to me than usual.

   _____

5. May I offer a <u>little</u> help?

   _____

6. He won't listen to any <u>advices</u>.

   _____

7. That hospital has too <u>much</u> patients and not enough beds.

   _____

8. There was a great <u>number</u> of asbestos at that school.

   _____

Answers begin on page 70.

Exercise 13 NOUN REVIEW

> **DIRECTIONS:** In each of the following sentences, four words or groups of words have been underlined. If one of these words is an error, blacken the space in the answer grid over the number corresponding to it. If there is no error in the sentence, blacken the space over number (5).

Example: We caught a large <u>number</u> of <u>fishes</u> due to <u>Raymond's</u>
$\quad\quad\quad$ 1 $\quad\quad\quad\quad\quad$ 2 $\quad\quad\quad\quad\quad$ 3
bringing the right <u>kind</u> of bait.
$\quad\quad\quad\quad\quad\quad\quad$ 4

○ ● ○ ○ ○
1 2 3 4 5

1. The <u>doorbell</u> <u>ringing</u> while I am taking a <u>bath</u> is an
$\quad\quad$ 1 $\quad\quad$ 2 $\quad\quad\quad\quad\quad\quad\quad\quad$ 3
annoying <u>disturbance</u>.
$\quad\quad\quad$ 4

1. ○ ○ ○ ○ ○
$\quad$ 1 2 3 4 5

2. Too <u>many</u> <u>furniture</u> makes the <u>walls</u> of this <u>room</u> seem to
$\quad\quad$ 1 $\quad\quad$ 2 $\quad\quad\quad\quad\quad$ 3 $\quad\quad\quad\quad$ 4
close in.

2. ○ ○ ○ ○ ○
$\quad$ 1 2 3 4 5

3. <u>John McEnroe's</u> tennis <u>playing</u> was good, but his
$\quad\quad\quad$ 1 $\quad\quad\quad\quad\quad\quad$ 2
<u>outbursts</u> disturbed his <u>opponent's</u> concentration.
$\quad\quad$ 3 $\quad\quad\quad\quad\quad\quad\quad$ 4

3. ○ ○ ○ ○ ○
$\quad$ 1 2 3 4 5

4. <u>Scissors</u>, paper, and <u>glue</u> were the <u>supplys</u> for the <u>class's</u>
$\quad$ 1 $\quad\quad\quad\quad\quad\quad$ 2 $\quad\quad\quad\quad$ 3 $\quad\quad\quad\quad$ 4
art project.

4. ○ ○ ○ ○ ○
$\quad$ 1 2 3 4 5

5. My two <u>brother-in-laws</u> have <u>degrees</u> from <u>universities</u> in
$\quad\quad\quad\quad$ 1 $\quad\quad\quad\quad\quad$ 2 $\quad\quad\quad$ 3
this <u>state</u>.
$\quad\quad$ 4

5. ○ ○ ○ ○ ○
$\quad$ 1 2 3 4 5

6. <u>Michael's</u> <u>return</u> set the <u>dogs</u> <u>tails</u> wagging.
$\quad$ 1 $\quad\quad$ 2 $\quad\quad\quad\quad$ 3 $\quad$ 4

6. ○ ○ ○ ○ ○
$\quad$ 1 2 3 4 5

7. Healthy <u>peoples'</u> <u>hair</u> and <u>nails</u> are always growing and
$\quad\quad\quad$ 1 $\quad\quad$ 2 $\quad\quad\quad$ 3
replacing themselves, but <u>teeth</u> cannot do this.
$\quad\quad\quad\quad\quad\quad\quad\quad\quad$ 4

7. ○ ○ ○ ○ ○
$\quad$ 1 2 3 4 5

8. White blood <u>cells</u> <u>function</u> is fighting <u>disease</u> and helping
$\quad\quad\quad\quad\quad$ 1 $\quad\quad$ 2 $\quad\quad\quad\quad\quad$ 3
<u>bodies</u> stay healthy.
$\quad$ 4

8. ○ ○ ○ ○ ○
$\quad$ 1 2 3 4 5

9. My <u>sister's</u> husband sells <u>radioes</u>, <u>stereos</u>, and CD
$\quad\quad$ 1 $\quad\quad\quad\quad\quad$ 2 $\quad\quad\quad$ 3
<u>players</u>.
$\quad$ 4

9. ○ ○ ○ ○ ○
$\quad$ 1 2 3 4 5

10. <u>Today's</u> <u>news</u> told of the <u>rebels'</u> <u>attackes</u> on the military
$\quad$ 1 $\quad\quad$ 2 $\quad\quad\quad\quad$ 3 $\quad\quad$ 4
targets.

10. ○ ○ ○ ○ ○
$\quad$ 1 2 3 4 5

11. My <u>wifes'</u> favorite <u>presents</u> were from her <u>sisters-in-law</u> and <u>half-brothers.</u>
    1   2   3
    4

11. ○ ○ ○ ○ ○
    1 2 3 4 5

12. While raking the front <u>lawn,</u> the two <u>teenagers</u> accumulated several <u>bagfuls</u> of <u>leafs.</u>
                          1   2
                                      3   4

12. ○ ○ ○ ○ ○
    1 2 3 4 5

13. <u>Bruce's</u> girlfriend stayed at her <u>mothers'</u> house when she caught the <u>measles</u> from the <u>children.</u>
    1   2
                    3   4

13. ○ ○ ○ ○ ○
    1 2 3 4 5

14. <u>Nancy's</u> <u>typing</u> is terrible; <u>Gloria's</u> is much faster because her <u>machine</u> is newer.
    1   2   3
            4

14. ○ ○ ○ ○ ○
    1 2 3 4 5

15. These <u>bikes</u> need special <u>wrenchs</u> to adjust their <u>brakes</u> and <u>gears.</u>
          1   2   3
              4

15. ○ ○ ○ ○ ○
    1 2 3 4 5

16. <u>John</u> <u>washing</u> the <u>clothes</u> in hot water was a <u>mistake.</u>
    1   2   3   4

16. ○ ○ ○ ○ ○
    1 2 3 4 5

17. <u>Bluejays,</u> beautiful <u>birds</u> to look at, are vicious <u>enemys</u> to many gentler <u>species</u> of birds.
    1   2   3
                            4

17. ○ ○ ○ ○ ○
    1 2 3 4 5

18. Last <u>night's</u> storm damaged many <u>homes</u> and several <u>pieces</u> of <u>equipments.</u>
         1   2
         3   4

18. ○ ○ ○ ○ ○
    1 2 3 4 5

19. <u>Shoes</u> and <u>sandal's</u> with leather <u>soles</u> feel best on my <u>feet.</u>
    1   2   3
    4

19. ○ ○ ○ ○ ○
    1 2 3 4 5

20. That <u>man</u> <u>singing</u> is a <u>joy</u> to my <u>ears.</u>
         1   2   3   4

20. ○ ○ ○ ○ ○
    1 2 3 4 5

21. The <u>child's</u> <u>problem</u> is a <u>result</u> of his two <u>parent's</u> abusiveness.
        1   2   3   4

21. ○ ○ ○ ○ ○
    1 2 3 4 5

22. Several committee <u>members</u> met to make a <u>list</u> of <u>criterias</u> for screening job <u>applicants.</u>
                      1   2
    3   4

22. ○ ○ ○ ○ ○
    1 2 3 4 5

23. During last <u>summer's</u> trip to the <u>children's</u> zoo, we fed a <u>family</u> of <u>deers.</u>
                1   2
    3   4

23. ○ ○ ○ ○ ○
    1 2 3 4 5

24. Some <u>instructors'</u> <u>class's</u> are interesting, but <u>others'</u> are duller than <u>sermons.</u>
         1   2   3
                                   4

24. ○ ○ ○ ○ ○
    1 2 3 4 5

25. That <u>business's</u> <u>sales</u> have decreased because <u>customers</u> are dissatisfied with its <u>products.</u>
         1   2   3
                                4

25. ○ ○ ○ ○ ○
    1 2 3 4 5

Answers begin on page 70.

Exercise 14   VERBS

A **verb** is a word that shows action:

study, think, write, run

A verb can also show a "state of being." The state of being verbs are:

am, is, are, was, were, being, been, be

A verb helps make a sentence by telling what the subject does or is.

Verb **tenses** set sentences in time periods. The three basic verb tenses are present, past, and future.

Anthony *works* for his family's bakery.

He *worked* in a factory before joining the family business.

He *will work* part time this winter while attending school.

DIRECTIONS: Underline the verbs in the sentences below. Some sentences have more than one verb.

Example: *Sofia traveled from Poland to the United States.*

1. Alonzo stirred the onions and garlic together.
2. Janice is your new supervisor.
3. We reported the accident to the police.
4. If the ladder slips, you will break your neck!
5. Your vote will decide the election.
6. Dana left early because she was ill.
7. Wisconsin is my favorite state.
8. Most mystery novels give clues throughout the story.
9. When the lights dimmed, the crowd booed.
10. When factories pour hot liquids into streams or lakes, they cause thermal pollution.
11. The driver behind us saw us, but he still hit the back end of our car.
12. Every time the door slams, Mattie jumps.
13. The cookies that you baked were delicious!
14. We spread the blanket for our picnic.
15. I write to my mother-in-law once a month.
16. I am the youngest child of six.
17. David thinks highly of you.
18. After you finish, take a break.

Answers begin on page 70.

Exercise 15   PAST TENSE REGULAR VERBS

1) Most verbs form their past tense in a regular manner by adding *ed:*

   rain, rained; arrest, arrested; listen, listened; annoy, annoyed

2) If the verb already ends in *e*, just add *d:*

   hope, hoped; demonstrate, demonstrated

3) If a short (one-syllable) verb ends in one vowel and one consonant, double the consonant before adding *ed:*

   hop, hopped; grab, grabbed; strut, strutted

4) If a longer verb ends in one vowel and one consonant *and* the last syllable is stressed, double the consonant before *ed:*

   permit, permitted; rebel, rebelled

5) If the stress is *not* on the last syllable, do *not* double the consonant:

   listen, listened; visit, visited

6) If a verb ends in *y* after a consonant, change *y* to *i* and add *ed:*

   copy, copied; marry, married

7) Add *ed* to most verbs ending in *y* after a vowel:

   play, played; annoy, annoyed

Note: Three common exceptions to this rule are *said, paid, laid.*

> **DIRECTIONS:** If there is an incorrect past form in the group of verbs, circle it. Then write the correct past form on the line. If all past forms are correct, write "OK" on the line.

Example: (visitted)	omitted	edited	*visited*
1. fanned	rainned	planned	_____
2. surveyed	stayed	carryed	_____
3. dropped	stopped	dripped	_____
4. rallied	emploied	emptied	_____
5. dryed	prayed	sprayed	_____
6. fastened	loosened	tightened	_____
7. scrubbed	cleaned	shined	_____
8. limited	visited	commited	_____

EXTRA PRACTICE:

Write five sentences about your life five years ago. Use the correct past forms of these verbs in your sentences: *enjoy, listen, hope, plan, worry.* (Do not write negative sentences.)

Examples: *Five years ago, I <u>listened</u> only to heavy metal. I <u>hoped</u> to be a rock star.*

Answers begin on page 70.

Exercise 16   PAST TENSE IRREGULAR VERBS

As you have seen, the past tense of most verbs is formed in a regular manner, by adding *ed:*

look, looked; pick, picked; rain, rained; jump, jumped

Some verbs, called **irregular verbs,** form the past tense differently:

bring, brought; eat, ate; come, came; sing, sang

To be certain of the correct past tense form of any irregular verb, you can check the dictionary.

> **DIRECTIONS:** Underline the correct past tense of each verb in parentheses.

Example: No one (weared, <u>wore</u>) a warm jacket.

1. Ryan (throwed, threw) the ball to the plate.
2. I (wrote, writ) a seven-page letter to Carlos.
3. When it got dark, we all (ran, run) home.
4. Gilda (slept, sleeped) until past noon.
5. The mail workers (striked, struck) for higher pay.
6. Yesterday, Diana Nyad (swam, swum) across the bay.
7. Lou (catched, caught) a cold on his camping trip.
8. The bird (flew, flied) over the rainbow.
9. Someone just (stoled, stole) a car from the parking lot.
10. The crowd (been, was) at the race since early afternoon.
11. The announcer (sayed, said) the show would go on.
12. Leonard and Doris (losed, lost) everything in the fire.
13. I really (feeled, felt) awful about their bad luck.
14. Everyone (saw, seen) the fireworks.
15. Ms. Johnson (teached, taught) math for twenty years.

EXTRA PRACTICE

Write five sentences about your first day of school this year or your first job. (Do not write negative sentences). Use the correct past tense forms of these verbs in your sentences:

feel	see
know	think
go	

Answers begin on page 70.

Exercise 17   ALL TENSES I

Besides the simple present, past, and future, there are other, more complicated tenses a verb can take.

In addition, one verb form—the **infinitive**—does not reflect different verb tenses. As its name implies, the infinitive is "timeless":

We like *to go* there. We wanted *to go* there last night. We plan *to go* there tomorrow.

> **DIRECTIONS:** Before each sentence below, the base form of the verb is written in parentheses. Decide on the correct form of the verb needed to fill in the blank in the sentence. Write the correct verb form in the blank.

Example: (bring) Has Lu _____brought_____ her boys to the class?

1. (eat) Have you _____ yet?

2. (see) Everyone had _____ the movie.

3. (go) When will you _____ to Washington?

4. (write) Davida decided _____ a letter to her boyfriend yesterday.

5. (write) Have you _____ down your Social Security number?

6. (get) A minute ago Mark _____ a flashlight so we could see.

7. (feel) I've never _____ so sick before.

8. (speak) Has the main character _____ yet?

9. (hurt) Ms. Miller just _____ herself on the rough edges of the desk.

10. (hear) We haven't _____ from the unemployment office.

11. (get) Has Khalil been able _____ his raise yet?

12. (break) How could the new car have _____ down already?

13. (sleep) Barry _____ on the sofa in the living room last night.

14. (leave) When my family _____ , I felt very lonely.

15. (freeze) The popsicles haven't _____ yet.

16. (do) What are you _____ ?

17. (drink) A baby will usually _____ a bottle of formula every four hours.

(continued)

18. (sweep) Don _____ the floor before his in-laws arrived.

19. (know) If I had _____ how late it was, I'd have stayed at home.

20. (think) Freddi promises she will _____ about our offer.

21. (do) Has Felipe _____ the project?

22. (buy) Although we had just _____ the drapes, they looked so awful we returned them.

23. (answer) The operator is _____ your call now.

24. (go) When you _____ to school, how large were your classes?

25. (sing) Verna and Mike have _____ in the choir for years.

26. (eat) I _____ the liver sausage pizza, and it was revolting.

27. (sit) I _____ so long that I was stiff.

28. (order) As soon as the waiter comes, we should _____ .

29. (take) The plane will be _____ off on time this morning.

30. (try) We are _____ to save money, but it's very difficult.

EXTRA PRACTICE

Write ten sentences as follows. Use correct verb forms.

1. List three things that you *have* accomplished so far this week.
   Example: *I have paid my phone bill.*

2. List two things that you *must* do today.
   Example: *I must go to the store.*

3. List two things that you *should have* done last week but didn't do.
   Example: *I should have sent a birthday card to my aunt.*

4. List three things that you *had* done by the time the guests arrived at your last party.
   Example: *I had vacuumed the carpet.*

Exercise 18 ALL TENSES II

When writing one or more paragraphs, be sure that your verb tenses are
correct. Pay attention to the context clues that tell you which tenses are
needed.

> **DIRECTIONS:** On each line, write the correct form of the verb in
> parentheses. (You may need to write more than one
> word.) Sometimes more than one answer is possible. An
> example is included.

Ever since childhood, I ___*have loved*___ traveling. And ever

1. (love)

since I _____ my first train trip at age eight, I

2. (take)

_____ riding trains more than any other form of

3. (enjoy)

transportation.

I still _____ that first train trip. At six in the

4. (remember)

morning, my father and I _____ the train in Gary,

5. (board)

Indiana, my hometown. I _____ the suitcase that I had

6. (carry)

_____ so carefully the night before. The conductor

7. (pack)

_____ us find seats, and he _____ me a

8. (help)   9. (give)

map of our route. I _____ so excited as I

10. (feel)

_____ all of the stops we'd make on our way to New

11. (see)

York. During the long trip, I didn't sleep at all. I just

_____ out the window at the cities, farms, and open

12. (look)

countryside that _____ by. I _____ only to

13. (flash)   14. (stop)

get some dinner in the dining car with my father. There was a

special menu for children, and I _____ every bite of

15. (eat)

my Loco-Burger.

(continued)

These days, I _____ not so interested in Loco-
     16. (be)

Burgers, especially since the train food _____
     17. (go)

downhill in recent years. However, I still _____
     18. (enjoy)

looking out the window as much as ever. I always

_____ calm and peaceful as I _____ at the
19. (feel)   20. (stare)

passing scenery. I _____ all my worries about school
     21. (forget)

and work and home.

Right now, I _____ a train trip south from New
     22. (plan)

York, where I currently _____ , to Mississippi. I am
     23. (live)

going _____ my cousins there, and we
     24. (visit)

_____ our annual family reunion. The trip
25. (attend)

_____ quite a few hours, as you can imagine, but I
26. (take)

_____ my time happily looking out the window and
27. (spend)

studying my route map. And will I eat Loco-Burgers? I think I

_____ about them and bring along my own food
28. (forget)

instead.

EXTRA PRACTICE

Write two paragraphs. In the first paragraph, describe a trip or an outing that
you took when you were a child. In the second paragraph, describe a trip or
an outing that you would like to take in the future. Use the following verbs in
both paragraphs:

go

see

do

bring

buy

Answers begin on page 70.

Exercise 19   VERB REVIEW

> **DIRECTIONS:** In each of the following exercises, four verbs have been underlined. If one of the verbs is used or formed incorrectly, blacken the space in the answer grid over the number corresponding to it. If all of the verbs are correct, blacken the space numbered (5).

Example: We <u>knew</u> we <u>should have went</u> slower, but we <u>wanted</u>
to <u>arrive</u> before dark.

   ○ ● ○ ○ ○
   1 2 3 4 5

1. Gabe <u>threw</u> the ball so hard it <u>hitted</u> the window and
    <u>broke</u> the glass, which <u>shattered</u> all over the ground.

    1. ○ ○ ○ ○ ○
        1 2 3 4 5

2. Federal Express <u>should have came</u> to pick up the
    package; if they <u>don't</u> <u>come</u> by noon, I <u>will deliver</u> it
    myself.

    2. ○ ○ ○ ○ ○
        1 2 3 4 5

3. When the mayor <u>became</u> engaged to marry, the
    newspapers <u>run</u> many articles about the couple—how they
    <u>met</u>, where they <u>went</u>, etc.

    3. ○ ○ ○ ○ ○
        1 2 3 4 5

4. <u>Will</u> you <u>make</u> a new pot of coffee? Someone <u>has drunken</u>
    all that was <u>left</u>.

    4. ○ ○ ○ ○ ○
        1 2 3 4 5

5. We <u>had run</u> a mile when we <u>noticed</u> that the fog had
    <u>crept</u> off the bay and <u>begun</u> to come inland.

    5. ○ ○ ○ ○ ○
        1 2 3 4 5

6. The Williamses <u>will send</u> their children to public school
    even though they <u>wish</u> they <u>are able</u> <u>to send</u> them to
    private school.

    6. ○ ○ ○ ○ ○
        1 2 3 4 5

7. Winter <u>has come</u> early this year. It <u>is</u> only October, and
    snow has <u>fallen</u> twice. The cold has <u>start</u> early too.

    7. ○ ○ ○ ○ ○
        1 2 3 4 5

(continued)

8. I <u>like</u> that sportscaster! You must <u>listen</u> to his program.
   ₁   ₂
   He <u>had</u> a sense of humor, and he <u>explains</u> the game well.
       ₃   ₄

   8. ◯ ◯ ◯ ◯ ◯
      1 2 3 4 5

9. When the shirt <u>was washt</u>, it <u>had</u> a white mark on it. I
             ₁   ₂
   <u>scrubbed and scrubbed</u>, but the mark <u>wouldn't come</u> off.
          ₃   ₄

   9. ◯ ◯ ◯ ◯ ◯
      1 2 3 4 5

10. Someone <u>rung</u> the doorbell and <u>spoiled</u> the peaceful
           ₁   ₂
    evening we <u>wished</u> we <u>could have had</u> by ourselves.
           ₃   ₄

    10. ◯ ◯ ◯ ◯ ◯
        1 2 3 4 5

11. The City Council <u>voted</u> <u>to end</u> the reduced bus fares on
                ₁   ₂
    Sundays. Since then, we <u>have had</u> <u>to paid</u> full fare for our
                          ₃   ₄
    shopping trips.

    11. ◯ ◯ ◯ ◯ ◯
        1 2 3 4 5

12. David <u>felt</u> proud. "I <u>done</u> my best!" he <u>said</u>, and <u>took</u> his
        ₁   ₂   ₃   ₄
    place in the winner's circle.

    12. ◯ ◯ ◯ ◯ ◯
        1 2 3 4 5

13. Itzhak Perlman <u>has become</u> a famous violinist. Although
                   ₁
    he <u>had</u> polio, which <u>left</u> him unable <u>to walk</u> without
       ₂   ₃   ₄
    braces, he performs all around the world.

    13. ◯ ◯ ◯ ◯ ◯
        1 2 3 4 5

14. North Americans <u>are</u> very health conscious; people <u>were</u>
              ₁   ₂
    careful about what they <u>eat</u>, and they <u>enjoy</u> many
                      ₃   ₄
    different types of exercise.

    14. ◯ ◯ ◯ ◯ ◯
        1 2 3 4 5

15. Has anyone <u>relieved</u> the doorman since he <u>begun</u> his
             ₁   ₂
    shift? He <u>looks</u> as if he might be <u>falling</u> asleep.
            ₃   ₄

    15. ◯ ◯ ◯ ◯ ◯
        1 2 3 4 5

16. The guide <u>had warned</u> us <u>to bring</u> warm clothing, so I
             ₁   ₂
    <u>brung</u> an extra coat and a pair of wool gloves that I
     ₃
    <u>had been saving</u>.
        ₄

    16. ◯ ◯ ◯ ◯ ◯
        1 2 3 4 5

Answers begin on page 71.

Exercise 20 SUBJECT AND VERB AGREEMENT

A subject and a verb are said to agree when the verb is in the right form for the subject. The chart below shows the right present tense verb form to use with subjects.

Singular Subjects		Plural Subjects	
I	like	We	like
You	like	You	like
He	likes	They	like
She	likes	They	like
It	likes	They	like

Example: *Juan drinks coffee, but his sisters drink tea.*

DIRECTIONS: In each sentence below, underline the correct verb form given in parentheses.

Example: *The tomatoes (are, is) not ripe yet.*

1. Many trees (shade, shades) the park.
2. Those pencils (need, needs) sharpening.
3. Lunch (are, is) on the table.
4. They (like, likes) science fiction stories.
5. She (drink, drinks) eight glasses of water a day.
6. Your shoes (have, has) gotten full of mud.
7. The employees (buy, buys) gifts for the boss's birthday.
8. The chairs (were, was) arranged in rows.
9. Rice (are, is) served in Vietnamese restaurants.
10. Problems (are, is) always coming up.
11. You (have, has) real musical talent.
12. The earth (revolve, revolves) around the sun.
13. Marcy (curl, curls) her own hair.
14. Beauticians (charge, charges) ten dollars to set your hair.
15. Two highways (meet, meets) near the college.
16. When you open the windows, sunlight (flood, floods) the room.
17. You (are, is) our last hope!
18. We (were, was) late for the movie.
19. I (take, takes) the train to work.
20. Drunk drivers (have, has) caused thousands of accidents.

Answers begin on page 71.

Exercise 21 AUXILIARIES AND *BEING* VERBS

Auxiliary, or helping, verbs are used in most questions and negative statements. For most tenses, these verbs must agree with their subjects. The verb *to be* must also agree with its subject in questions and negatives.

Does Ken know how to cook? No, he *doesn't* know how.
Were you asleep when I called? No, I *wasn't* asleep.

DIRECTIONS: In each sentence, the auxiliary verb has been underlined. If it is correct, write "OK" above the verb. If it is incorrect, cross it out and write the correct form of the verb above it.

---

haven't
Example: We ~~haven't~~ seen that movie yet.

1. <u>Are</u> he a talented musician?

2. The children <u>doesn't</u> eat anything but spaghetti.

3. <u>Do</u> your mother drive to work?

4. <u>Has</u> those people decided how to vote yet?

5. Anthony <u>weren't</u> able to attend the concert.

6. <u>Was</u> Mr. Kim working at the front desk when you arrived?

7. In my view, she <u>don't</u> need to lose any more weight.

8. Why <u>is</u> you staring at me so intently?

9. <u>Has</u> Ed and Sue left for vacation?

10. <u>Aren't</u> the flowers beautiful?

11. <u>Is</u> the Joneses going to attend?

12. They <u>isn't</u> planning to go.

13. <u>Does</u> Joan and Will own a car?

14. Unfortunately, I <u>do</u> not know the answer.

15. <u>Do</u> either of you want more coffee?

EXTRA PRACTICE

Think about yourself and a friend. Write a total of six sentences:

Write two sentences that begin with *I don't* . . .

Write two sentences that begin with *She doesn't* . . . or
He doesn't . . .

Write two sentences that begin with *We don't* . . .

Answers begin on page 71.

Exercise 22   PHRASES AND GERUNDS

In some sentences it is harder to choose the correct verb form. Follow the rules below.

1) Sometimes a phrase or clause separates the subject and verb. To make sure the verb agrees with the subject, *ignore* the interrupting words and focus only on the simple subject.

   The *coffee* in the cups *is* getting cold.

2) A gerund can be the subject of a sentence. Always use a singular verb with a gerund subject.

   Listening to tapes *relaxes* me.

DIRECTIONS: In each sentence below, write the correct present tense form of the verb in parentheses.

Example: (be) Walking, as well as other exercises,

_____*is*_____ good for the heart.

1. (provide) Green vegetables, as well as fruit, _____ vitamin C.

2. (be) This film about the endangered monkeys _____ interesting.

3. (be) The seats in the front row of the theater _____ empty.

4. (belong) The tools in the carton on the porch _____ to the janitor.

5. (cost) A set of new tires _____ more than I can pay.

6. (take) Grading homework assignments _____ up much of a teacher's free time.

7. (be) The bills from his accident on the job _____ being paid by the workmen's compensation program.

8. (be) "Taking drugs _____ a sure way to mess up your life," said the former cocaine abuser.

EXTRA PRACTICE

Copy and complete each sentence using *is* or *are* (or another present tense verb).

Example: Drinking alcohol . . .

   Drinking alcohol is foolish if you plan to drive.

Smoking cigarettes . . .

The drugs that people buy on the street . . .

Answers begin on page 71.

34

Exercise 23   INVERTED SENTENCES

1) In sentences in which the verb comes before the subject (inverted word order), you must be sure to find the subject and decide if it is singular or plural.

In that apartment *live* four young *women*.

2) Sentences that begin with *here* or *there* are also in inverted order. You must find the true subject of these kinds of sentences to determine the form of the verb.

Here *is* the *reason* for the delay.

There *are* the *coconuts*.

DIRECTIONS: In each sentence below, underline the correct verb given in parentheses.

Example: There (are, is) several items on the agenda.

1. Here (are, is) the best single answer to all your questions.
2. Enclosed (are, is) two copies of my transcripts.
3. In the Nicolet Forest (grow, grows) many kinds of fir trees.
4. There (were, was) hundreds of unhappy ticketholders turned away from the concert.
5. In Jake's record collection (are, is) all of Bruce Springsteen's albums.
6. There (weren't, wasn't) a soul out on the street.
7. Where (are, is) my keys?
8. At the back of the book (are, is) a glossary.
9. There (go, goes) another twenty-dollar bill!
10. On the floor (were, was) dozens of ants.
11. From the mountains (come, comes) the cold weather.
12. Here (come, comes) the new tenants.
13. There (are, is) a bagel and a bialy left.
14. What (do, does) he do for a living?
15. At the end of the movie (are, is) a car chase and a crash.
16. Here (are, is) the copies you requested.
17. Why (do, does) LuAnn and Ronnie insist upon turning up the volume of the radio?
18. There (sit, sits) two of the best card players.

Answers begin on page 71.

Exercise 24   COLLECTIVE NOUNS

Learn the rules and study the examples below for making verbs agree with problem subjects.

1) Use the verb form for a singular subject when the subject is a collective noun which is thought of as a single unit:

   The *crowd is* breaking up now.

   If the collective noun is meant to refer to each of the group's members, use the verb form for a plural subject:

   The *staff have* to get flu shots.

2) Some nouns may look plural but are actually singular. Be sure to use the verb form for a singular subject with nouns like these:

   Mathematics is always hard for me.

3) Amounts and measurements used as subjects usually require the verb form for singular subjects:

   Eight hours is too long to drive.

> **DIRECTIONS:** In each sentence below, underline the correct verb given in parentheses.

Example: *Three weeks (are, is) a generous vacation.*

1. The news (were, was) depressing after the earthquakes.
2. Two inches (were, was) cut off Syril's hair.
3. Physics (are, is) hard for most students.
4. The doctor says that my diabetes (are, is) controllable.
5. Civics (have, has) always interested me.
6. The faculty often (disagree, disagrees) about grading policies.
7. Five dollars (have, has) to last me until next Friday.
8. Economics (weren't, wasn't) taught when I was a student.
9. (Are, Is) the basketball team well trained?
10. The band (play, plays) popular music.
11. The staff (take, takes) off different days so someone is always on duty.
12. Measles (cause, causes) a red, itching rash.
13. Nine months (seem, seems) so long to be pregnant!
14. The United States (have, has) over 240 million people.
15. The audience (were, was) applauding enthusiastically.

Answers begin on page 71.

Exercise 25   INDEFINITE PRONOUNS

Some indefinite pronouns are always considered to be singular, even though they may seem plural in meaning.

Each of the boys *is* in charge of *his* own suitcase.

Below is a list of indefinite pronouns that are always considered to be singular.

each	one	someone	somebody	something	nothing
either	no one	anyone	anybody	anything	
neither	everyone	nobody	everybody	everything	

Other indefinite pronouns can be either singular or plural depending on the meaning they get from another word in the sentence:
   Some of the *eggs are* cracked.
   Some of the *milk is* for breakfast.

All, any, some, none, more, and *most* are indefinite pronouns that can be either singular or plural.

DIRECTIONS: In each sentence below, underline the correct verb form given in parentheses.

Example: *Everyone (want, wants) dessert.*

1. One of the problems (are, is) our lack of free time.
2. Everyone (use, uses) her own paintbrushes.
3. Most of the boys (come, comes) from Texas.
4. Neither of the drugs (help, helps) a sore back.
5. All of the authors (sign, signs) their books at the sale.
6. Most of the clothing at the flea market (look, looks) torn and dirty.
7. Any of the plans (are, is) acceptable.
8. (Have, Has) either of the cabins been rented?

EXTRA PRACTICE

Complete the following sentences in the present tense. Be sure your verbs agree with your subjects.

   Nothing in my closet . . .

   Everything I wear . . .

   Each of my shirts . . .

   All of my clothes . . .

Answers begin on page 71.

Exercise 26   COMPOUND SUBJECTS I

A compound subject joined by *and* is usually considered to be plural.

Cookies and donuts are very fattening.

With a compound subject joined by *or, either/or,* or *neither/nor,* make the verb agree with the part of the subject nearer to the verb:

Either some squirrels or a *dog keeps* spilling our garbage.

DIRECTIONS: In each sentence below, underline the correct verb form given in parentheses.

Example: Neither Bess nor her sisters (play, plays) piano.

1. Pansies and geraniums (grow, grows) well in window boxes.
2. Long underwear and heavy jackets (keep, keeps) the forest rangers warm.
3. Either some earthquakes or a volcano (shake, shakes) this area from time to time.
4. Either the television or the radio (are, is) on.
5. Parents and their children (are, is) invited.
6. A doctor or a paramedic (are, is) licensed to give oxygen.
7. The animals or their keeper (leave, leaves) the gates open.
8. Horses and a sleigh (are, is) needed to get around on this ice.
9. The lights or the iron (use, uses) enough electricity to blow a fuse.
10. Both the problems and the solution (are, is) printed in the workbook.
11. Fried chicken and spaghetti (are, is) his favorite foods.
12. I don't recall if the Ochoas or their daughter (were, was) there.
13. A breeze and some clouds (are, is) spoiling our picnic.
14. Neither the windows nor the door (have, has) been left open.
15. The cheese, magarine, and milk (have, has) been refrigerated.

Answers begin on page 71.

Exercise 27 COMPOUND SUBJECTS II

A compound subject joined by *not only . . . but also* takes the verb form for either a singular or plural subject depending on the part of the subject nearer to the verb.

Not only the typewriter but also the file *cabinets were* moved.

Be careful with sentences that have a predicate nominative. The verb always agrees with the subject, not the predicate nominative:

A popular *breakfast is* ham and eggs.

DIRECTIONS: Underline the correct verb form for the sentence.

Example: Not only your sweater but also your jeans (<u>are</u>, is) full of holes.

1. Not only Leila but also her brothers (are, is) able to attend the luncheon.

2. Not only my parents but also my grandmother (are, is) eager to meet you.

3. "Patience and perseverence (are, is) the answer," said the school counselor.

4. My favorite meal (are, is) ribs and fries with barbecue sauce.

5. Not only the clock in the living room but also the one in the kitchen (tell, tells) the right time.

6. Not only the trains rattling by but also the noise from next door (have, has) given me a tremendous headache.

7. If your problem (are, is) drugs, seek help immediately.

8. Not only the teenage boy but also his parents (were, was) unable to quit smoking; they were all addicted.

EXTRA PRACTICE

Complete the sentences using the correct form of present tense verbs.

Example: Either the bus or a taxi . . .

> *Either the bus or a taxi is an easy way to get to the museum.*

Cars and buses . . .

Either the bus or the train . . .

Neither trains nor buses . . .

Answers begin on page 71.

Exercise 28   RELATIVE PRONOUNS

In adjective, or relative, clauses the pronouns *who, that,* and *which* can be singular or plural depending on the nouns they modify. Be sure the verb in the clause agrees with the singular or plural pronoun.

The *child who lives* next door is very bright.

child = singular

I am one of those *people that are* afraid to fly.

people = plural

DIRECTIONS: Write the correct form of the verb in parentheses.

Example: *(need) John is a boy who* _____*needs*_____ *a lot of attention.*

1. (open) This is an umbrella that _____ automatically.

2. (burn) This is one of those toasters that _____ everything to a crisp within seconds.

3. (own) The Richardsons, who _____ the house next door, have been wonderful neighbors.

4. (prefer) Shawn is a person who __*preferes*__ reading to partying.

5. (need) Our car, which desperately __*need*__ a tune-up, is sitting in the parking lot.

6. (admire) One of the few people that still _____ Dr. Kringle is his son, Dexter.

7. (sleep) Do you know the identity of the man who always _____ in front of that grocery store at night?

8. (include) "Geraldo" is one of several television shows that _____ audience participation.

EXTRA PRACTICE

Copy and complete each sentence using the present tense. Use the correct verb form.

Example: *My teacher is a person that . . .*

My teacher is a person that cares about young people.

I am someone who . . .

I am one of the few people that . . .

40

Exercise 29 AGREEMENT REVIEW

DIRECTIONS: In each sentence below, underline the correct verb form given in parentheses.

Example: The windows and the floor (<u>need</u>, needs) washing.

1. The curtains (don't, doesn't) close completely.
2. Everybody in the cast (have, has) rehearsal tonight.
3. Every day, either Ashley or her parents (visit, visits) Mrs. Cousins.
4. He (don't, doesn't) understand English well.
5. A bowl of ice cream with nuts (were, was) our snack.
6. The problem of rats and roaches in abandoned buildings (are, is) hard to solve.
7. Gail is one of those people who (cause, causes) grief wherever she goes.
8. One of those programs (were, was) supposed to be shown on television last night.
9. On the picnic table (were, was) sandwiches, potato chips, and soda pop.
10. The man that (claim, claims) to be a reporter is lying.
11. The jury (haven't, hasn't) reached a verdict.
12. Someone around here (don't, doesn't) use deodorant!
13. The family always (eat, eats) at six o'clock.
14. Crime in the cities (make, makes) me afraid to go out at night.
15. The scissors (need, needs) sharpening.
16. Each nurse (have, has) his or her own station.
17. Parachuting from airplanes (are, is) not my idea of fun.
18. Here (grow, grows) the freshest vegetables in town.
19. Three miles (are, is) the distance to the factory.
20. Robert Cray and his bass player (sound, sounds) great on the CD.

21. Neither the chemical additives nor the disgusting filling (make, makes) me want to eat those cupcakes.

22. Not only string beans but also corn (add, adds) vitamins to your diet.

23. Some of those items (sell, sells) rapidly.

24. Constructing model cars (are, is) Gene's hobby.

25. Half of the cars on the road today (are, is) economy-sized models.

26. The neighbors on our block (are, is) friendly.

27. She (don't, doesn't) believe your excuse.

28. (Was, Were) there any tickets left when you got there?

29. Under the mat (are, is) the keys to both locks.

30. I sometimes give money to homeless people who (say, says) they are hungry.

31. Writing essays (are, is) a lot of fun.

32. (Do, Does) each of you have a book?

33. Neither of the men (want, wants) dessert.

34. Some of the speech (need, needs) revising.

35. Please let me know if there (are, is) any problems.

36. A candy bar and a glass of orange juice (were, was) my lunch.

37. By the bookcase (are, is) a stack of file folders.

38. A light jacket or a sweater (are, is) warm enough.

39. I want one of those pens that (have, has) erasable ink.

40. If any of the pages (are, is) missing, please let me know.

41. If any of the page (are, is) missing, please let me know.

42. In my opinion, fifty dollars (are, is) too much to pay for a paperback book.

43. Either the supervisor or her assistant (interview, interviews) job candidates.

44. Here (lie, lies) the laziest cat in the entire world!

45. Eating pizza and other spicy foods (give, gives) me heartburn.

Answers begin on page 72.

42

Exercise 30 PRONOUNS

A **pronoun** is a word that can replace a noun:

When the pilots completed their basic training, *they* had a party.

In using pronouns, remember these things:
1) Choose correctly either subjective, objective, reflexive, or possessive forms.
2) Choose the right number and person to match the noun being replaced.
3) Use the correct form and spelling of the pronoun.

> **DIRECTIONS:** Underline the correct pronoun form given in parentheses.

Example: The finest mathematician is (she, her).

1. Calvin sent (we, us) a secret message.
2. (Our, Ours) flashlight needs new batteries.
3. We need (you, your) signature.
4. This locker is (mine, mines).
5. There is a telephone call for (she, her).
6. Michael painted the kitchen (hisself, himself).
7. Give (you, yourself) a pat on the back!
8. Darkness frightens (I, me).
9. (I, Me) found some plums in the refrigerator.
10. Do (you, yourself) know the way to the auditorium?
11. Janet and Tanya drove home (herselves, themselves).
12. The Kleins' apartment is smaller than (ours, our's).
13. Those shoes are (hers, her's).
14. (We, Us) are going fishing.
15. Jeff lent his fishing pole to (us, ourselves).
16. Jackie gave (he, him) a kiss.
17. The boys pay for the insurance (theirselves, themselves).
18. The prizes were (theirs, their's).
19. Minnie wants your address for (her, herself's) records.
20. (He, Himself) was the fastest swimmer.
21. Please give the package to (he, him).
22. Do (they, them) have an answering machine?

Answers begin on page 72.

Exercise 31   COMPOUNDS AND PRONOUNS

1) Sometimes nouns and/or pronouns are joined by *and, nor,* or *or.* In cases like these, read the sentence without the "extra" noun or pronoun to decide upon the correct forms:

> Their parents and (they, them) get along well.
> (Their parents get along well. *They* get along well.)

> (She, Her) and (I, me) have the same perfume.
> (*She* has the same perfume. *I* have the same perfume.)

2) Remember to use the objective form after prepositions:

> It was a problem for Deborah and (I, me).
> (It was a problem for Deborah. It was a problem for *me.*)

DIRECTIONS: Underline the correct pronoun form of the two given.

Example: Ernesto and (I, me) will read the report.

1. Mike and (I, me) work well together.
2. (We, Us) and (they, them) are distant relatives.
3. The loggers and (they, them) sleep in the bunk house.
4. (He, Him) and his motorcycle make me nervous.
5. Jason's grandmother used to knit beautiful sweaters for his sister and (he, him).
6. The instructor showed Hiroshi and (they, them) the answers to the test.
7. With you and (she, her) by my side, I am not afraid.
8. Darlene and (he, him) have been seeing each other in secret.
9. (They, Them) and (we, us) do not get along easily.
10. Just between you and (I, me), I've noticed Steve spends a lot of time on the office phone.
11. Jimmy tried to protect the other children and (we, us) from the gangs.
12. Extra assignments were given to David and (I, me).

EXTRA PRACTICE

Write six complete sentences using these phrases correctly:

my family and I, my family and me, they and we, them and us, you and I, you and me.

Answers begin on page 72.

Exercise 32   *WHO* AND *WHOM*

In formal English, *who* and *whoever* are used only as subjects. The pronouns *whom* and *whomever* are used as objects.

Whoever leaves last must lock the door.

Our leader, *whom* we admire, will be speaking soon.

DIRECTIONS: Using formal English, write *who* or *whom*.

Example: Do you see _____*who*_____ *is sitting in the front row?*

1. _____ have you chosen to play the part?

2. _____ knows the combination to the safe?

3. The doctor _____ I saw last week answered all my questions.

4. My sister, _____ collects souvenir plates, has just returned from a plate auction.

5. The librarian to _____ I spoke referred me to the reference desk.

6. Parents _____ respond quickly to their babies' cries are giving them a sense of trust and security.

7. Can you tell me _____ I should consult regarding health benefits?

DIRECTIONS: Using formal English, write *whoever* or *whomever*.

---

8. Marry _____ you please—it is no concern of mine.

9. _____ needs assistance should notify the representative at the blue desk.

10. I know that _____ teaches you will appreciate your positive attitude.

11. You will endanger _____ you inform.

12. _____ has found the missing jewels should step forward immediately.

Answers begin on page 72.

Exercise 33 *TO BE* AND COMPARISONS

Follow these rules to choose the right kind of pronoun:

1) After any form of the verb *to be,* use the subjective form of the pronoun:

   It was *she* who provided the documents.

2) After the words *than* or *as,* supply the missing part of the sentence to determine whether to use the subjective or objective pronoun form:

   Eric is definitely smarter than *he* (is).

   The officers know my brother better than *me.*
   (better than they know me)

> **DIRECTIONS:** Underline the correct pronoun form of the two given.

Example: Toni Morrison is as good a writer as (her, <u>she</u>).

1. Do you think Daryl Hannah is prettier than (I, me)?
2. The first caller was (she, her).
3. Dan spends more time with the TV than with (I, me).
4. The goalie weighs twenty pounds less than (he, him).
5. Some countries are not as advanced as (we, us) in the area of fighting cancer.
6. Paula Abdul sings that better than (she, her).
7. Their family has more money than (we, us).
8. The best dancers are (he, him) and (she, her).
9. Our best runner has always been (he, him).
10. If you were (she, her), would you attempt the dive?
11. When Dr. Jacobs retired, we found a new dentist, and we liked her as much as (he, him).
12. Sharon has more patience than (they, them).

EXTRA PRACTICE

Compare yourself to *one* other person (a brother or sister, mother or father, friend, etc.). Write sentences using the following phrases. Use the correct pronoun forms after the word *than.*

Example: <u>My friend Rosie</u> is a better cook than <u>I.</u>

1. . . . a better cook than . . .
2. . . . a better dancer than . . .
3. . . . a bigger sports fan than . . .
4. . . . a harder worker than . . .

Answers begin on page 72.

Exercise 34 APPOSITIVES, REFLEXIVES, POSSESSIVES

3) When *we* or *us* is followed by a noun, mentally leave out the noun to see if the pronoun is used as a subject or object:

    We New Yorkers move fast. (We . . . move fast.)

    The children called *us* foreigners bad names. (The children called us . . . bad names.)

4) Reflexive pronouns, which end in *self or selves,* are used when the subject's "self" receives the action:

    He was proud of *himself.*

    Do not use a reflexive pronoun when a subjective or objective pronoun is needed.

5) Use the possessive form of a pronoun before a gerund:

    His snoring kept everyone awake.

DIRECTIONS: Underline the correct pronoun form of the two given.

Example: I am tired of (you, your) complaining.

1. (Your, You) tampering with the equipment has led to a malfunction.

2. An actress and (myself, I) rehearsed the lines.

3. My supervisor won't tolerate (me, my) smoking on the job.

4. (We, Us) senior citizens don't get a fair deal.

5. The government should send (we, us) taxpayers a refund.

6. Will (me, my) singing disturb you?

7. Glenda and (I, myself) don't get along too well.

8. City people think (we, us) small town folk are dumb.

9. No one likes (you, your) complaining about the situation.

10. The animal rights activist did not appreciate (him, his) wearing a fur coat.

11. (We, Us) voters have a lot of power.

12. Call (we, us) servicemen whenever there's trouble.

13. Florence and (yourself, you) are late.

14. (We, Us) teenagers are often misunderstood.

15. Don't blame (we, us) men for all of women's problems.

16. Dana and (he, himself) plan to be married.

17. (You, Your) hammering has given (me, myself) a headache.

18. (We, Us) workers demand stricter safety regulations.

19. (We, Us) adults returning to school need special help.

20. I plan to buy (me, myself) a new coat.

Answers begin on page 72.

Exercise 35   NUMBER AND PERSON I

1) When the pronoun replaces two or more nouns joined by *and*, use the plural form of the pronoun:

   Leon and *Bob* rode *their* motorcycles through town.

2) When the pronoun replaces two nouns joined together by *or, nor, either . . . or, neither . . . nor,* or *not only . . . but also,* the pronoun agrees with the last noun in the series:

   Not only the dogs but also the *cat* found *its* own food.

3) When the pronoun replaces a collective noun, use a singular pronoun if the noun is thought of as a single unit. Use a plural pronoun if the noun is thought of as separate people or things:

   The *faculty* is top-notch; *its* reputation is unmatched.

   The *staff* are doing *their* paperwork now.

DIRECTIONS: Underline the correct pronoun of the two given.

Example: *Not only the fenders but also the chrome trim has lost (its, their) shine.*

1. Barbara and her children lost (her, their) lease.

2. Not only the residents but also the owner asked for (his, their) apartment to be painted.

3. The group holds (its, their) meetings at noon.

4. Not only hot soup but also fresh bread sent (its, their) aroma down the stairs.

5. The family are taking (its, their) showers now.

6. In my opinion, the movies and television have lost (its, their) appeal because of the violence in them.

7. The crowd showed (its, their) approval by clapping.

8. The circus clowns and the ringmaster took (his, their) bows.

9. The table or the chairs need (its, their) positions changed.

10. Either the fudge or the chocolate brownies left (its, their) mark on my waistline!

11. The orchestra tune up (its, their) instruments before each performance.

12. Neither the employees nor the president wore (her, their) usual business attire on the day the company moved.

Answers begin on page 72.

Exercise 36   NUMBER AND PERSON II

Use the singular form of the pronoun with these words:

person	neither	someone	somebody
each	no one	anyone	anybody
either	everyone	nobody	everybody

Also use the singular form of the pronoun with all other compounds beginning with *any, every, no,* and *some:*

> Neither of the men brought *his* ticket.

> Everything should be in *its* own place.

> **Note:** Many writers now use the singular phrases *his or her* or *him or her* with singular nouns and pronouns that could refer to either males or females:

> A *manager* should try to develop the talents of *his or her* staff.

> If *anyone* wants a refund, give it to *him or her.*

> **DIRECTIONS:** If there is an error in a sentence, correct the error on the line provided. If a sentence is correct, write "OK" on the line.

Example: *Everyone must control their temper.*

Everyone must control his or her temper.

1. No one should abuse their body that way.

   _____

2. Nobody can cope with her own problems better than my sister.

   _____

3. The company is looking for an applicant who has their own car.

   _____

4. If neither of the men wants their dessert, I'll eat both sundaes.

   _____

5. When an employee works hard, the company should reward them.

   _____

6. Someone parked their car in my parking place.

   _____

7. Each of the plans has its advantages.

   _____

8. If anyone calls me while I am on vacation, please tell them that I will be back on Friday.

   _____

Answers begin on page 72.

Exercise 37   PRONOUNS REVIEW

DIRECTIONS: If there is an error in a sentence, blacken the space in the answer grid over the number corresponding to it. If there is no error, blacken the space numbered (5).

Example: President Kennedy said we citizens should help our
                              1   2
country by aiding in its development and by improving
                          3
our own physical fitness.
4

◯ ◯ ◯ ◯ ●
1 2 3 4 5

1. Us Californians don't like your calling us crazy the way
   1   2   3
   you do.
   4

   1. ◯ ◯ ◯ ◯ ◯
      1 2 3 4 5

2. People who have problems sometimes need help from
          1
   someone whom can listen to them and offer his or her
          2   3   4
   advice.

   2. ◯ ◯ ◯ ◯ ◯
      1 2 3 4 5

3. Can you do this yourself, or should I call someone who
       1   2   3   4
   can help?

   3. ◯ ◯ ◯ ◯ ◯
      1 2 3 4 5

4. It was me who encouraged you to interview at my
          1   2   3   4
   company.

   4. ◯ ◯ ◯ ◯ ◯
      1 2 3 4 5

5. Call me when you need a hand with those tires of your's,
        1   2   3
   and I'll come right over.
       4

   5. ◯ ◯ ◯ ◯ ◯
      1 2 3 4 5

6. Neither Matilda nor her sister brought their own skis.
                       1   2
   They expect to use ours.
   3   4

   6. ◯ ◯ ◯ ◯ ◯
      1 2 3 4 5

7. It could not have been he who answered your call.
   1   2 3   4

   7. ◯ ◯ ◯ ◯ ◯
      1 2 3 4 5

8. We secretaries are underpaid. Nobody works as hard as
   1   2
   us, yet none of us has gotten a raise.
   3   4

   8. ◯ ◯ ◯ ◯ ◯
      1 2 3 4 5

9. Them are the ones whom we elected to our Congress.
   1   2   3   4

   9. ◯ ◯ ◯ ◯ ◯
      1 2 3 4 5

10. Everyone who came to the party thanked Ben and I for
    1   2   3
    inviting him or her.
             4

    10. ◯ ◯ ◯ ◯ ◯
        1 2 3 4 5

(continued)

50

11. It upsets <u>me</u> when <u>someone</u> like <u>yourself</u> doesn't do
    $\quad\;\;$ 1 $\qquad\qquad$ 2 $\qquad\;\;$ 3
    <u>his or her</u> share of work.
    $\quad$ 4

    11. ○ ○ ○ ○ ○
    $\quad$ 1 $\;$ 2 $\;$ 3 $\;$ 4 $\;$ 5

12. Not only <u>I</u> but also <u>my</u> sons have packed <u>their</u> bags and
    $\qquad\quad$ 1 $\qquad\quad$ 2 $\qquad\qquad\qquad$ 3
    put <u>them</u> in the car.
    $\quad\;$ 4

    12. ○ ○ ○ ○ ○
    $\quad$ 1 $\;$ 2 $\;$ 3 $\;$ 4 $\;$ 5

13. <u>We</u> instructors don't mind <u>you</u> studying together for the
    $\;$ 1 $\qquad\qquad\qquad\quad$ 2
    test; <u>you</u> can help each other prepare for <u>it</u>.
    $\qquad$ 3 $\qquad\qquad\qquad\qquad\qquad$ 4

    13. ○ ○ ○ ○ ○
    $\quad$ 1 $\;$ 2 $\;$ 3 $\;$ 4 $\;$ 5

14. <u>His</u> wife and <u>him</u> ordered <u>us</u> teenagers off <u>their</u> property.
    $\;$ 1 $\qquad\quad$ 2 $\qquad\quad$ 3 $\qquad\qquad\quad$ 4

    14. ○ ○ ○ ○ ○
    $\quad$ 1 $\;$ 2 $\;$ 3 $\;$ 4 $\;$ 5

15. <u>You</u> and <u>she</u> are taller than <u>him</u> or <u>I</u>.
    $\;\;$ 1 $\qquad$ 2 $\qquad\qquad\quad$ 3 $\quad$ 4

    15. ○ ○ ○ ○ ○
    $\quad$ 1 $\;$ 2 $\;$ 3 $\;$ 4 $\;$ 5

16. The girls and <u>I</u> met Maelean, <u>whom</u> <u>we</u> had heard about
    $\qquad\qquad$ 1 $\qquad\qquad\quad$ 2 $\quad$ 3
    from <u>you</u>.
    $\qquad$ 4

    16. ○ ○ ○ ○ ○
    $\quad$ 1 $\;$ 2 $\;$ 3 $\;$ 4 $\;$ 5

17. <u>We</u> parents resent <u>him</u> interfering with how <u>we</u> raise <u>our</u>
    $\;$ 1 $\qquad\qquad$ 2 $\qquad\qquad\qquad$ 3 $\qquad$ 4
    children.

    17. ○ ○ ○ ○ ○
    $\quad$ 1 $\;$ 2 $\;$ 3 $\;$ 4 $\;$ 5

18. Dr. Lang says <u>us</u> runners may have <u>our</u> own special
    $\qquad\qquad$ 1 $\qquad\qquad\qquad$ 2
    problems with <u>our</u> feet when <u>we</u> age.
    $\qquad\qquad$ 3 $\qquad\quad$ 4

    18. ○ ○ ○ ○ ○
    $\quad$ 1 $\;$ 2 $\;$ 3 $\;$ 4 $\;$ 5

19. This is the medicine for <u>yourself</u>; <u>you</u> must take <u>it</u> for
    $\qquad\qquad\qquad\quad$ 1 $\qquad$ 2 $\qquad\quad$ 3
    <u>your</u> high blood pressure.
    $\;$ 4

    19. ○ ○ ○ ○ ○
    $\quad$ 1 $\;$ 2 $\;$ 3 $\;$ 4 $\;$ 5

20. Yvette and <u>I</u> are grateful to Dr. Roussos. It was <u>her</u> <u>who</u>
    $\qquad\quad$ 1 $\qquad\qquad\qquad\qquad\qquad\qquad\qquad$ 2 $\;\;$ 3
    recommended <u>us</u> for the job.
    $\qquad\qquad$ 4

    20. ○ ○ ○ ○ ○
    $\quad$ 1 $\;$ 2 $\;$ 3 $\;$ 4 $\;$ 5

21. When the sewers backed up into <u>our</u> basements, <u>we</u>
    $\qquad\qquad\qquad\qquad\qquad$ 1 $\qquad\qquad$ 2
    homeowners complained to <u>whoever</u> would listen to <u>us</u>.
    $\qquad\qquad\qquad\qquad$ 3 $\qquad\qquad\qquad$ 4

    21. ○ ○ ○ ○ ○
    $\quad$ 1 $\;$ 2 $\;$ 3 $\;$ 4 $\;$ 5

22. <u>Someone</u> <u>who</u> loves <u>their</u> children will usually raise <u>them</u>
    $\quad$ 1 $\qquad$ 2 $\qquad$ 3 $\qquad\qquad\qquad\qquad\qquad$ 4
    correctly.

    22. ○ ○ ○ ○ ○
    $\quad$ 1 $\;$ 2 $\;$ 3 $\;$ 4 $\;$ 5

23. <u>Whomever</u> speaks ill of <u>her</u> must deal with <u>him</u> and <u>me</u>.
    $\quad$ 1 $\qquad\qquad$ 2 $\qquad\qquad\quad$ 3 $\qquad$ 4

    23. ○ ○ ○ ○ ○
    $\quad$ 1 $\;$ 2 $\;$ 3 $\;$ 4 $\;$ 5

24. These pens use up <u>their</u> ink quickly; the problem with
    $\qquad\qquad$ 1
    <u>them</u> is that <u>you</u> can't see how much ink is left in <u>it</u>.
    $\;$ 2 $\qquad$ 3 $\qquad\qquad\qquad\qquad\qquad\qquad$ 4

    24. ○ ○ ○ ○ ○
    $\quad$ 1 $\;$ 2 $\;$ 3 $\;$ 4 $\;$ 5

25. Sylvie and <u>I</u> warned Marc to be careful when using the
    $\qquad\quad$ 1
    electric saw, but <u>he</u> didn't heed <u>our</u> warning and hurt
    $\qquad\qquad\quad$ 2 $\qquad\qquad$ 3
    <u>hisself</u>.
    $\;$ 4

    25. ○ ○ ○ ○ ○
    $\quad$ 1 $\;$ 2 $\;$ 3 $\;$ 4 $\;$ 5

Answers begin on page 72.

Exercise 38 ADJECTIVES AND ADVERBS

An **adjective** is a word that describes a noun to tell what kind, which one, or how many:

This was the *first* medicine to relieve *allergy* symptoms for *twelve* hours.

An **adverb** is a word that modifies a verb, an adverb, or an adjective to tell how, when, where, or to what extent:

Yesterday, we met *there very briefly* to discuss the report.

> **DIRECTIONS:** Draw an arrow from the underlined word to the word it modifies. Then, on the line provided, tell whether the underlined word is an adjective or an adverb.

Example: A <u>tall</u> man called for you.   _____*adjective*_____

1. Your suit is <u>very</u> stylish.   1. _____

2. <u>Some</u> flowers seem to attract bees more than others.   2. _____

3. The <u>orange</u> blanket belongs in the back bedroom.   3. _____

4. The coach eats that <u>instant</u> cereal I see advertised on TV.   4. _____

5. The chairs scraped <u>noisily</u> on the floor when we stood up.   5. _____

6. <u>Salted</u> peanuts cost $2 a bag.   6. _____

7. The detective crept <u>cautiously</u> out of his hiding place.   7. _____

8. Come <u>here</u> and let me see you.   8. _____

9. Let's go to the laundromat <u>now</u>.   9. _____

10. There are <u>several</u> movies that are worth seeing.   10. _____

11. We finished the bread <u>today</u>.   11. _____

12. <u>Lukewarm</u> water is best for most washing.   12. _____

13. A <u>careless</u> person broke the fragile antique chair.   13. _____

14. Jan was <u>truly</u> sorry to be late for the wedding.   14. _____

15. The hijacking victims were <u>extremely</u> frightened, but not hurt.   15. _____

Answers begin on page 72.

52

Exercise 39 ADVERBS

The rules below will help you to spell adverbs correctly.

1) Most adverbs are formed by adding *ly* to the adjective:

   quiet, quietly; careful, carefully

2) Adjectives that end in *y* after a consonant are made into adverbs by changing the *y* to *i* and adding *ly:*

   easy, easily; happy, happily

3) Adjectives that end in *le* are usually made into adverbs by changing the ending to *ly:*

   probable, probably; possible, possibly

4) Adjectives that end in *ll* are made into adverbs by adding *y:*

   dull, dully; full, fully

5) Adjectives that end in *ic* are usually made into adverbs by adding *ally:*

   historic, historically; frantic, frantically

6) Some adjectives that end in *ly* remain the same when used as adverbs:
   daily, early

7) Some adjectives not ending in *ly* stay the same when used as adverbs:
   fast, late, hard, far, long

8) Some adjectives cannot be used as adverbs:
   lonely, friendly

9) Some adverbs have special spellings:
   truly, publicly, wholly

> **DIRECTIONS:** If there is an incorrect adverb form in the group of adverbs, circle it and write the correct spelling on the line. If all adverb forms are correct, write "OK."

Example: *gently*   (basicly)   *wickedly*   *undoubtedly*   _basically_

1. safely	extremely	freely	positivley	_____
2. possiblely	probably	daily	dully	_____
3. secretly	importantly	definitly	tightly	_____
4. publicly	historicly	economically	realistically	_____
5. lamely	expensively	tamely	truely	_____
6. guiltily	badly	finaly	seriously	_____
7. coldly	coolly	warmly	hotly	_____
8. happily	mightily	messyly	coyly	_____
9. strangly	peculiarly	foolishly	dangerously	_____
10. early	sincerly	fairly	marvelously	_____

Answers begin on page 73.

Exercise 40 PREDICATE ADJECTIVES

Use an adjective after forms of the verb *to be* and other verbs that do not show action. An adjective in this position is called a **predicate adjective:**

The weather has been *bad* all week.

She looks *good.*

Note: Usually the word *well* is used as an adverb:

Damaris writes very *well.*

There is one exception to this rule. Use *well* as an adjective when referring to someone's health:

I have not been *well* since I caught the flu.

> **DIRECTIONS:** Underline the correct form of the two given in parentheses.

Example: Gina felt (<u>bad,</u> badly) about her mistake.

1. The day looks (good, well) for our picnic.
2. The rotten eggs smell (awful, awfully).
3. I cut myself (bad, badly) on the sharp edge of the can.
4. I feel so (sore, sorely) I can't move.
5. Rachel sews (good, well).
6. The children became (noisy, noisily) on the long bus ride.
7. They behaved (good, well) at the museum, however.
8. The book is (easy, easily) for most students.
9. Sharona looked (beautiful, beautifully) in her bathing suit.
10. Pedro looked (good, well) in his suit, too.
11. His arms felt (strong, strongly) as he carried me to safety.
12. She always grows (nervous, nervously) on Sunday night.
13. The doctor says I will be (good, well) by tomorrow.
14. Your cooking always smells so (good, well).
15. Our cat can't smell (good, well) enough to catch a mouse.
16. Your shirt looks (dirty, dirtily).
17. That girl appears (familiar, familiarly) to me.
18. When will you be (ready, readily)?
19. Do you feel (healthy, healthily) enough to travel?
20. The days become noticeably (short, shortly) in the fall.

(continued)

54

21. Jared feels (eager, eagerly) about his new hobby.

22. I'm pleased that you're feeling (alert, alertly) so soon after your operation.

23. He (brave, bravely) tasted the pickled frog legs.

24. I have never been so (proud, proudly) of my wife as I am today.

25. A down coat will keep you quite (warm, warmly) during the cold winter months.

26. After this watermelon, everything else tastes (sour, sourly).

27. That candidate has an advantage in the election; she looks so (good, well) on television.

28. No one felt as (angry, angrily) as Pete when he got the layoff notice.

29. Be sure to look (careful, carefully) before you cross the street.

30. Almost any news sounds (well, good) when you're far away from home.

EXTRA PRACTICE

Each of the pairs of words below has a verb and an adjective or adverb. Write sentences using these pairs of words correctly. Be sure to check the forms of both the verb and the adjective or adverb you use.

Examples: taste/daintily

Aunt Tillie <u>daintily tasted</u> the cucumber sandwich.

taste/delicious

Coffee <u>tastes delicious</u> with a touch of cinnamon.

look/quickly

look/good

grow/quickly

grow/tired

feel/gently

feel/wonderful

Answers begin on page 73.

Exercise 41   NEGATIVE ADVERBS

1) The adverb *not* can combine with auxiliary verbs such as *is* and *have* to make contractions such as *isn't* and *haven't*. The word *ain't* is not acceptable in formal or written English.
2) When you use such negative adverbs as *never, hardly, scarcely, rarely, seldom,* and *not* (or contractions made with *n't*), do not use any other negatives in the sentence.

> I did*n't* buy any food there.
>
> (NOT: I did*n't* buy *no* food there.)

DIRECTIONS: Underline the correct word for the sentence.

Example: We never touched (<u>any,</u> none) of the money.

1. He (ain't, hasn't) received any news yet.
2. Julie and David Chen don't have (any, no) children yet.
3. I'm the wrong person to ask; I know (anything, nothing) about it.
4. That child (has, hasn't) hardly touched her food.
5. The president (ain't, isn't) about to change his stand on abortion.
6. Professor McKenna (has, hasn't) seldom come to class unprepared.
7. I was alone that evening; (anyone, no one) was with me.
8. So far, we (have, haven't) received no response to our inquiry.
9. In my opinion, Leticia (isn't, ain't) confident enough in her own abilities.
10. Mr. Banerji (can, cannot) rarely take a vacation from his busy job.
11. Rachel has hardly (any, no) sympathy for her brother's drinking problem.
12. No gift has (ever, never) touched me as much as yours has.

EXTRA PRACTICE

Write five sentences using these words:

hardly

never

scarcely

seldom

Answers begin on page 73.

Exercise 42   *THIS/THAT, THESE/THOSE, A/AN*

1) Use the adjective *this* for singular nouns that are close by. Use the adjective *that* for singular nouns that are some distance away:

> I prefer *this* seat by the door.

> Can you see *that* car in the lot?

2) Use *these* for plural nouns that are close by.
Use *those* for plural nouns that are some distance away.

> *These* shoes kill my feet.

> *Those* railroad tracks need repairing.

3) Never say *this here* or *that there*.
Never use the objective pronoun *them* to point to something.

4) Use *an* before words that begin with a vowel sound. For all other words, use *a:*

> *an* eagle; *a* heated argument, *an* hour

For words that begin with *u* or *eu* pronounced like *you*, use *a:*

> *a* usual event; *a* eulogy

> **DIRECTIONS:** In each sentence, one or more words or phrases are underlined. If an underlined word or phrase is incorrect, cross it out and write the correct word above it. If there is no mistake, write "OK."

Example: *Observe this̶ ̶h̶e̶r̶e̶ reaction in the test tube.* (this)

1. <u>These</u> woman is innocent of all charges.

2. Charles attends <u>an</u> university in Georgia.

3. Do you believe the governor is <u>an</u> honest man?

4. What are <u>this</u> books doing on my desk?

5. Mrs. Begay has made <u>a</u> outstanding contribution to her field.

6. I'd appreciate it if you'd take <u>them</u> newspapers in the garage to the recycling center.

EXTRA PRACTICE

Write a sentence for each group of words or phrases. Use *all* of the words in your sentence. Important: Use *a* or *an* correctly before each of the words or phrases in the group.

1) politician—honest person

2) encyclopedia—useful resource—assignment in that class

3) university—unique opportunity—education

Answers begin on page 73.

Exercise 43   ADJECTIVE/ADVERB COMPARISONS I

Whenever you use an adjective or an adverb to compare two or more nouns or pronouns, use the form that is correct for the number of things being compared:

1) To show that two persons, things, groups, or actions are unequal, use the *er* ending, or add the word *more* or *less:*

   Today is *warmer* than yesterday.

   You walk *more quickly* than Florence.

   Courtney is *less cooperative* than his brother.

2) To show that one person, thing, group, or action stands out from a group of three or more, use the *est* ending, or add *most* or *least:*

   Genevieve is the *cleverest* person I know.

   Of the three sisters, Ellen is the *most talented.*

   Bones is the *least playful* dog I've ever seen.

> **DIRECTIONS:** Underline the correct form of the adjective or adverb in parentheses.

Example: *She is the (nicer, nicest) of the twins.*

1. Which was the (smaller, smallest) of the Seven Dwarfs?
2. Which class is (harder, the hardest): math or English?
3. Leontyne Price sings (more beautifully, the most beautifully) than any other living opera star.
4. We had the (stranger, strangest) experience of our lifetimes last night.
5. Midge is (less patient, the least patient) than I.
6. Lake Thompson is (deeper, the deepest) of all the lakes around the Rhinelander.
7. Which live (longer, the longest) as pets: goldfish or turtles?
8. John Kennedy was one of the (more popular, most popular) presidents.
9. Of the two brothers, Doug is the (more eager, most eager) to graduate.
10. This is the (rainier, rainiest) April we have ever had.

Answers begin on page 73.

Exercise 44 ADJECTIVE/ADVERB COMPARISONS II

3) Use only one form of comparison, not two:

Jan is *smarter* than her sister.
(NOT: *more smarter*)

4) Long adjectives (three or more syllables) and adverbs that end in *ly* are usually not used with an *er* or *est* ending:

Gran is *more impatient* than ever.
(NOT: *impatienter*)

5) Some adjectives and adverbs have irregular forms:

This coffee tastes *better* than mine.
(NOT: *gooder*)

I am the *worst* singer in the world!
(NOT: *worstest*)

DIRECTIONS: Fill in the blank with the correct adjective or adverb form of the word underlined in each sentence.

Example: In Japan, Yoko is a <u>popular</u> girl's name, but Yasuko is <u>*more popular.*</u>

1. I felt <u>bad</u> before, but I feel even _____ now.

2. You may be <u>hungry,</u> but I am definitely the _____ person in this family.

3. Because of the excellent faculty, King High students go <u>far</u>—much _____ than students in other high schools.

4. Today is <u>hot</u>, but tomorrow is predicted to be the _____ day of the year.

5. The ads say this cereal has <u>more</u> raisins than other brands, but I think the store brand has the _____ raisins of all.

6. If you think Melvin is <u>ugly</u>, you should see his brother; he is much _____ .

7. Nurses handle babies <u>gently</u>, but new mothers handle them the _____ of all.

8. Cathy wants <u>curly</u> hair; this permanent promises the _____ hair possible from a kit.

9. Ann is <u>heavy</u>, but she used to be even _____ .

10. Decimal problems are <u>easier</u> than fractions, but whole numbers are the _____ problems of all.

11. Jerry is <u>tall</u>, but he is not the _____ boy in his class.

12. The snow is <u>deep</u> now, and it will be even _____ in a few hours.

13. I have only a <u>few</u> debts, but my sister has even _____ debts than I do.

14. All doctors work <u>carefully</u>, but surgeons must work the _____ of all doctors.

15. That record sounds <u>good</u>, and this one sounds a little _____ .

16. Many guests were <u>late</u>, but our next-door neighbors were the _____ of all.

17. Detroit is <u>far</u> from our town; it is _____ than we can drive in one day.

18. You thought you were <u>poor</u>? The people upstairs are the _____ people I have ever known.

19. Yesterday was <u>rainy</u>, and today is _____ .

20. The seam on your dress is <u>uneven</u>. Now you have made it worse! It is _____ than it was before.

EXTRA PRACTICE

Write three sentences comparing two family members.

Example: *My sister is <u>more musical</u> than I.*

Write three sentences telling why a famous person stands out from others in his or her profession:

Example: *Arsenio Hall is the <u>most interesting</u> talk show host on TV because he jokes with his guests.*

Answers begin on page 73.

Exercise 45   ADJECTIVE/ADVERB REVIEW

> **DIRECTIONS:** In each of the following sentences, four words have been underlined. If one of these words is incorrectly used in the sentence, blacken the space in the answer key over the number corresponding to it. If all of the words are used correctly, blacken the space numbered (5).

Example: Yesterday Scott didn't look well, and today he feels
1   2   3
badly.
4

   ○ ○ ○ ● ○
   1 2 3 4 5

1. New Orleans is more close to Miami than Atlanta, but I'd
                   1
rather drive farther and be able to visit my best friends
           2   3
there.
4

  1. ○ ○ ○ ○ ○
      1 2 3 4 5

2. Of the two little boys, Josh was the taller, but Daniel was
          1   2
definitely the more mature.
3   4

  2. ○ ○ ○ ○ ○
      1 2 3 4 5

3. Mario sings good, Luis sings even better, and Theresa
           1   2   3
sings the best of all.
       4

  3. ○ ○ ○ ○ ○
      1 2 3 4 5

4. Eat less calories and you will soon weigh less and have
     1   2   3
more energy.
4

  4. ○ ○ ○ ○ ○
      1 2 3 4 5

5. Don had a good time skating, but he didn't wear nothing
         1   2
on his head, so his ears quickly got cold.
                   3   4

  5. ○ ○ ○ ○ ○
      1 2 3 4 5

6. Freddi is obviously brighter than her boss, who insists
         1   2
that all employees follow instructions exact as she gives
     3   4
them.

  6. ○ ○ ○ ○ ○
      1 2 3 4 5

7. Tonight was so darkly that we couldn't see farther than
  1   2 3   4
three feet.

  7. ○ ○ ○ ○ ○
      1 2 3 4 5

8. Visit us soon; we'll be real glad to show you around.
      1   2   3   4

  8. ○ ○ ○ ○ ○
      1 2 3 4 5

9. We have hardly caught no fish for an hour.
    1   2   3   4

  9. ○ ○ ○ ○ ○
      1 2 3 4 5

10. Using illegal drugs is a extremely dangerous practice.
      1   2   3   4

  10. ○ ○ ○ ○ ○
      1 2 3 4 5

11. If you keep making <u>nasty</u> remarks, you will <u>soon</u> be
    known as the <u>meanest</u> person <u>here.</u>

    11. ○ ○ ○ ○ ○
       1 2 3 4 5

12. I am <u>truly</u> <u>happily</u> that you appreciate <u>fine</u> cooking and
    <u>leisurely</u> dining.

    12. ○ ○ ○ ○ ○
       1 2 3 4 5

13. Joe's comments are <u>awful</u> <u>insensitive;</u> you'd think he'd be
    <u>more careful</u> than he <u>usually</u> is.

    13. ○ ○ ○ ○ ○
       1 2 3 4 5

14. The doorbell's <u>loud</u> ringing disturbed us just before we
    fell asleep. It was <u>very</u> <u>hard</u> to become <u>sleepily</u> again.

    14. ○ ○ ○ ○ ○
       1 2 3 4 5

15. <u>This</u> exercises were <u>long,</u> but they were not <u>especially</u>
    <u>difficult.</u>

    15. ○ ○ ○ ○ ○
       1 2 3 4 5

16. If you <u>don't</u> take the medicine <u>daily,</u> you will <u>gradually</u>
    feel <u>worser.</u>

    16. ○ ○ ○ ○ ○
       1 2 3 4 5

17. I <u>surely</u> regret repeating <u>that</u> rumor; if I had known it
    would make you feel <u>badly,</u> I <u>wouldn't</u> have repeated it.

    17. ○ ○ ○ ○ ○
       1 2 3 4 5

18. Masho <u>sharply</u> turned the wheel of his car to avoid
    hitting <u>an</u> old dog walking <u>slowly</u> across the road, but his
    car <u>unexpected</u> nicked a tree.

    18. ○ ○ ○ ○ ○
       1 2 3 4 5

Answers begin on page 73.

62

Final Skills Inventory GRAMMAR AND USAGE

> **DIRECTIONS:** In each of the following sentences, four words or groups of words have been underlined. If one of these is an error in grammar or usage, blacken the space in the answer key over the number corresponding to it. If there is no error, blacken the space numbered (5).

Example: <u>She's</u> a much better vocalist than <u>me,</u> but I still enjoy <u>singing</u> with
      1   2   3

    <u>her.</u>
     4

                                                      ○ ● ○ ○ ○
                                                      1 2 3 4 5

1. <u>Shoes</u> often <u>conforms</u> to the <u>feet</u> of the person <u>who</u> wears them.
    1   2   3   4

    1. ○ ○ ○ ○ ○
         1 2 3 4 5

2. <u>Have</u> the child <u>read</u> both of <u>her</u> <u>stories</u> to the class?
    1   2   3 4

    2. ○ ○ ○ ○ ○
         1 2 3 4 5

3. The <u>weatherman</u> <u>said</u> he <u>predicted</u> a cloudy day and <u>was</u> surprised
         1   2   3   4

    by the sunshine.

    3. ○ ○ ○ ○ ○
         1 2 3 4 5

4. I wanted to <u>buy</u> one of <u>those</u> <u>radios</u> that <u>comes</u> with earphones.
              1   2   3   4

    4. ○ ○ ○ ○ ○
         1 2 3 4 5

5. <u>Us</u> prisoners were <u>afraid</u> the warden would poison <u>us</u> with <u>spoiled</u>
    1   2   3   4

    food.

    5. ○ ○ ○ ○ ○
         1 2 3 4 5

6. The <u>fish</u> <u>bited</u> the bait and was <u>caught</u> <u>easily.</u>
       1   2   3   4

    6. ○ ○ ○ ○ ○
         1 2 3 4 5

7. The <u>firefighters</u> <u>came</u> <u>quick</u> in response to our <u>frantic</u> calls.
        1   2   3   4

    7. ○ ○ ○ ○ ○
         1 2 3 4 5

8. Someone <u>mistakenly</u> <u>took</u> <u>my</u> coat instead of <u>theirs.</u>
            1   2 3   4

    8. ○ ○ ○ ○ ○
         1 2 3 4 5

9. The announcer <u>whom</u> <u>read</u> the <u>tragic</u> news was <u>badly</u> shaken.
               1   2   3   4

    9. ○ ○ ○ ○ ○
         1 2 3 4 5

10. <u>Who</u> told <u>you</u> to <u>whom</u> the gift was to be <u>sent?</u>
     1   2   3   4

    10. ○ ○ ○ ○ ○
          1 2 3 4 5

11. Many people were hurt when the dam bursted.
    <u>1</u> <u>2</u>   <u>3</u>   <u>4</u>

    11. ○ ○ ○ ○ ○
        1 2 3 4 5

12. We haven't found hardly any time to spend on ourselves.
    1 2   3   4

    12. ○ ○ ○ ○ ○
        1 2 3 4 5

13. If either of the stolen watchs is found, I will be surprised.
    1   2   3   4

    13. ○ ○ ○ ○ ○
        1 2 3 4 5

14. It cost least to repair our car than to buy a new one.
    1   2   3   4

    14. ○ ○ ○ ○ ○
        1 2 3 4 5

15. Kate has been real relaxed since the baby's health improved.
    1   2   3

    15. ○ ○ ○ ○ ○
        1 2 3 4 5

16. It don't pay to eat at home these days.
    1   2   3   4

    16. ○ ○ ○ ○ ○
        1 2 3 4 5

17. All of the photos in them albums are from high school.
    1   2   3   4

    17. ○ ○ ○ ○ ○
        1 2 3 4 5

18. Neither the driver nor his passengers wants to stop for lunch.
    1   2   3   4

    18. ○ ○ ○ ○ ○
        1 2 3 4 5

19. When darkness fell, we had took our tents out, but had not pitched
    1   2   3   4

    them yet.

    19. ○ ○ ○ ○ ○
        1 2 3 4 5

20. Angelas job, as well as her childcare duties, seems to be too much
    1   2   3   4

    for her.

    20. ○ ○ ○ ○ ○
        1 2 3 4 5

21. Do you ever ask yourself whom is in charge of your children on the
    1   2   3   4

    school bus?

    21. ○ ○ ○ ○ ○
        1 2 3 4 5

22. Neither Marlene nor Jessica plays as well as you or me.
    1   2   3   4

    22. ○ ○ ○ ○ ○
        1 2 3 4 5

23. After five minutes' practice on the ice, I had fell ten times.
    1   2 3 4

    23. ○ ○ ○ ○ ○
        1 2 3 4 5

24. People who complain earn themselves a bad reputation.
    1   2   3   4

    24. ○ ○ ○ ○ ○
        1 2 3 4 5

25. You drinking so much beer is surely a threat to your health.
    1   2   3   4

    25. ○ ○ ○ ○ ○
        1 2 3 4 5

(continued)

26. The salad contains lettuce, <u>tomatos</u>, <u>olives</u>, <u>mushrooms</u>, and bean
₁ ₂ ₃

    <u>sprouts</u>.
₄

    26. ○ ○ ○ ○ ○
       1 2 3 4 5

27. <u>Pinching</u> <u>pennies</u> <u>are</u> a way of life in our house; <u>saving</u> is always
₁ ₂ ₃ ₄

    encouraged.

    27. ○ ○ ○ ○ ○
       1 2 3 4 5

28. Only one of the <u>guests</u> <u>offered</u> to <u>clean</u> up after <u>themselves</u>.
₁ ₂ ₃ ₄

    28. ○ ○ ○ ○ ○
       1 2 3 4 5

29. Everyone in the car pool <u>drives</u> <u>much</u> faster than <u>me</u> but never <u>has</u>
₁ ₂ ₃ ₄

    an accident.

    29. ○ ○ ○ ○ ○
       1 2 3 4 5

30. New types of scalpels cut <u>more</u> <u>cleanly</u> and cause <u>fewer</u> <u>bleeding</u>
₁ ₂ ₃ ₄

    than metal scalpels.

    30. ○ ○ ○ ○ ○
       1 2 3 4 5

31. Joe's <u>running</u> around without gloves <u>led</u> to <u>his</u> getting frostbite.
₁ ₂ ₃ ₄

    31. ○ ○ ○ ○ ○
       1 2 3 4 5

32. "<u>Whose</u> number <u>hasn't</u> been <u>call</u> yet?" asked the <u>salesperson</u>.
₁ ₂ ₃ ₄

    32. ○ ○ ○ ○ ○
       1 2 3 4 5

33. Relations between <u>Ed's</u> aunt and <u>he</u> have been bad since the two of
₁ ₂

    <u>them</u> argued about <u>his</u> smoking.
₃ ₄

    33. ○ ○ ○ ○ ○
       1 2 3 4 5

34. One of the <u>most popular</u> bands <u>is</u> New Kids on the Block, but I <u>have</u>
₁ ₂ ₃

    never heard <u>none</u> of their albums.
₄

    34. ○ ○ ○ ○ ○
       1 2 3 4 5

35. Chuck looked <u>so</u> <u>confidently</u> that we were sure <u>he</u> had <u>won</u> the case.
₁ ₂ ₃ ₄

    35. ○ ○ ○ ○ ○
       1 2 3 4 5

36. The rat that <u>run</u> down the alley hadn't <u>eaten</u> <u>any</u> of the <u>poison</u>.
₁ ₂ ₃ ₄

    36. ○ ○ ○ ○ ○
       1 2 3 4 5

37. <u>Who</u> <u>sings</u> <u>best</u>: Charlotte or <u>I</u>?
₁ ₂ ₃ ₄

    37. ○ ○ ○ ○ ○
       1 2 3 4 5

38. <u>Grandma's</u> three <u>daughter-in-laws</u> and their <u>children</u> visit her on
₁ ₂ ₃

    <u>holidays</u>.
₄

    38. ○ ○ ○ ○ ○
       1 2 3 4 5

39. My <u>sisters-in-law</u> have <u>less</u> problems with my brothers than <u>we</u> in
₁ ₂ ₃

    the family <u>do</u>.
₄

    39. ○ ○ ○ ○ ○
       1 2 3 4 5

40. Of <u>all</u> the <u>people</u> on the block, the Jeffersons <u>seem</u> <u>happier</u>.
      1   2   3   4

40. ○ ○ ○ ○ ○
   1 2 3 4 5

41. <u>Can</u> someone <u>from</u> the main office <u>deliver</u> the package <u>themselves</u>?
  1   2   3   4

41. ○ ○ ○ ○ ○
   1 2 3 4 5

42. This <u>is</u> <u>an</u> unique chance to show how <u>well</u> you can <u>compete</u>.
      1 2   3   4

42. ○ ○ ○ ○ ○
   1 2 3 4 5

43. <u>Your</u> taking the medicine <u>daily</u> will <u>quickly</u> make you <u>well</u>.
  1   2   3   4

43. ○ ○ ○ ○ ○
   1 2 3 4 5

44. The <u>most small</u> pets I have ever seen are "Sea Monkeys." <u>They</u> are
         1   2

really <u>tiny</u> shrimp.
  3   4

44. ○ ○ ○ ○ ○
   1 2 3 4 5

45. The <u>peoples'</u> <u>dreams</u> <u>were</u> the same as <u>ours</u>.
      1   2   3   4

45. ○ ○ ○ ○ ○
   1 2 3 4 5

46. The <u>historic</u> event was recorded <u>immediately</u> and <u>permanent</u> for
       1   2   3

future <u>generations</u>.
       4

46. ○ ○ ○ ○ ○
   1 2 3 4 5

47. One of the people <u>whom</u> I know <u>the best</u> <u>is</u> my <u>husband's</u> sister.
               1   2   3   4

47. ○ ○ ○ ○ ○
   1 2 3 4 5

48. Joan <u>doesn't</u> look <u>nicely</u> today, but she should look <u>better</u> <u>soon</u>.
       1   2   3   4

48. ○ ○ ○ ○ ○
   1 2 3 4 5

49. The manager <u>told</u> Mel and <u>I</u> that <u>our</u> work is <u>excellent</u>!
             1   2   3   4

49. ○ ○ ○ ○ ○
   1 2 3 4 5

50. Yesterday, <u>those</u> <u>policewomen</u> <u>arrived</u> at the scene the <u>most quickest</u>
             1   2   3   4

of all the police officers.

50. ○ ○ ○ ○ ○
   1 2 3 4 5

Answers and Explanations begin on page 67.

FINAL SKILLS INVENTORY EVALUATION CHART

> **DIRECTIONS:** After completing the Final Skills Inventory, check your answers by using the Final Skills Inventory Answers and Explanations, pages 67–68. Write the total number of your *correct* answers for each skill area in the blank boxes below. If you have *more than one incorrect* answer in any skill area, you need more practice. Exercises to study in this workbook are listed in the last column.

Skill Area	Item Number	Total	Number Correct	Exercise Numbers
Plural Nouns	13, 26, 38	3	_____	6–9
Possessive Nouns	20, 45	2	_____	10–11
Countable and Uncountable Nouns	30, 39	2	_____	12
Verb Tenses	6, 11, 19, 23, 32, 36	6	_____	15–18
Subject-Verb Agreement	1, 2, 4, 16, 18, 27	6	_____	20–28
Pronoun Case	5, 9, 21, 22, 25, 29, 33, 49	8	_____	30–34
Pronoun Number and Person	8, 28, 41	3	_____	35–36
Adjective Form	17, 35, 42, 48	4	_____	38, 40, 42
Adverb Form	7, 15, 46	3	_____	38–41
Negative Adverbs	12, 34	2	_____	41
Adjective Comparison	37, 40, 44	3	_____	43–44
Adverb Comparison	14, 50	2	_____	43–44

(NO ERROR: Items 3, 10, 24, 31, 43, 47)

Note: A score of 33 or more correct is considered passing for this Inventory.

Answers and Explanations   FINAL SKILLS INVENTORY

> **DIRECTIONS:** After completing the Final Skills Inventory, use these Answers and Explanations to check your work. *On these pages,* circle the number of each item you correctly answered. Then turn to the Final Skills Inventory Evaluation Chart and follow the instructions given.

1. **(2)** The verb form *conform* is needed because the simple subject *Shoes* is plural.

2. **(1)** The auxiliary *Has* is needed because the simple subject *child* is singular.

3. **(5)** No error

4. **(4)** The pronoun *that* is plural because it refers to *radios.* Therefore, the plural verb *come* is needed.

5. **(1)** The subjective pronoun *We* is needed.

6. **(2)** The correct past tense of the verb *bite* is *bit.*

7. **(3)** The adverb *quickly* is needed to tell how the firefighters came.

8. **(4)** The singular pronouns *his or hers* should be used to refer to *someone,* which is singular.

9. **(1)** The subjective form *who* is needed as the subject of the verb *read.*

10. **(5)** No error

11. **(4)** The correct past tense of the verb *burst* is *burst.*

12. **(2)** The correct auxiliary is *have.* The adverb *hardly* is negative, so there should not be any other negatives in the sentence.

13. **(3)** The correct plural of *watch* is *watches.*

14. **(2)** The correct adverb for comparing two unlike verbs is *less. Least* can only be used to compare three or more things.

15. **(2)** The adverb form *really* is needed to tell *to what extent* Kate has been relaxed.

16. **(1)** The verb form *doesn't* is needed because the subject *It* is singular.

17. **(2)** The objective pronoun *them* can never be used as an adjective. The correct word is *those.*

18. **(4)** The verb form *want* is needed to agree with the closer subject *passengers,* which is plural. In a *neither . . . nor* sentence, the verb should agree with the subject nearer to the verb.

19. **(3)** The correct past participle form is *taken.*

20. **(1)** The correct possessive form of *Angela* is *Angela's.*

21. **(3)** The subjective form *who* is needed as the subject of the verb *is.*

22. **(4)** The subjective form *I* is needed. The sentence really means that the others don't play as well as *I* play.

(continued)

23. **(4)** The correct past participle form is *fallen*.

24. **(5)** No error

25. **(1)** The possessive form *Your* is needed before the gerund *drinking*.

26. **(1)** The correct plural of *tomato* is *tomatoes*.

27. **(3)** The simple subject is the gerund *Pinching*, which takes the verb form for a singular subject.

28. **(4)** The singular pronouns *himself* or *herself* are needed because the pronoun refers to *one*, which is singular.

29. **(3)** The subjective pronoun *I* is needed to express the comparison that everyone drives faster than *I* drive.

30. **(3)** The adjective *less* is needed because *bleeding* is an uncountable noun.

31. **(5)** No error

32. **(3)** The correct past participle form is *called*.

33. **(2)** The objective pronoun form *him* is needed because it is the object of the preposition *between*.

34. **(4)** The positive form *any* is needed because the sentence already has a negative *(never)*.

35. **(2)** The adjective form *confident* is needed after the nonaction verb *looked*.

36. **(1)** The past tense *ran* is needed.

37. **(3)** The adverb form *better* is needed because only two people are being compared.

38. **(2)** The correct plural is *daughters-in-law*.

39. **(2)** The adjective *fewer* is needed because *problems* is a countable noun.

40. **(4)** The adjective form *happiest* is needed because more than two people are being compared.

41. **(4)** The singular pronouns *himself* or *herself* are needed to refer to *someone*, which is singular.

42. **(2)** The adjective *a* is needed because the word *unique* begins with a *you* sound.

43. **(5)** No error

44. **(1)** The correct adjective form is *smallest*. It shows comparison among three or more things.

45. **(1)** The correct possessive form is *people's* because the plural noun *people* does not end in *s*.

46. **(3)** The adverb form *permanently* is needed. It tells how the event was recorded.

47. **(5)** No error

48. **(2)** The adjective form *nice* is needed after the nonaction verb *look*.

49. **(2)** The objective pronoun *me* is needed; the subject is *manager*.

50. **(4)** The adverb form *most quickly* should be used to tell how and when the policewomen arrived.

Complete the Final Skills Inventory Evaluation Chart on page 66.

ANSWER KEY

EXERCISE 1

1. dentist works
2. weight-lifters practiced
3. drivers have been
4. center opens
5. mother is moving
6. partner will deliver
7. creams prevent
8. David left
9. chef prepared
10. article moved

EXERCISE 2

1. S	11. F
2. F	12. S
3. F	13. F
4. F	14. S
5. S	15. F
6. S	16. F
7. F	17. S
8. F	18. F
9. S	19. S
10. F	20. F

EXERCISE 3

1. (you) Leave
2. you Have met
3. alarm will ring
4. tire is
5. (you) Climb
6. Alex did quit
7. (you) bring
8. anyone Can read
9. (you) Abandon
10. floor could be
11. (you) Turn
12. solution is
13. you Did enjoy
14. hamburgers Are
15. (you) Wash

EXERCISE 4

1. 4	10. 2
2. 1	11. 3
3. 5	12. 5
4. 2	13. 1
5. 1	14. 4
6. 3	15. 5
7. 5	16. 2
8. 1	17. 3
9. 3	18. 5

EXERCISE 5

1. 2	5. 1
2. 2	6. 3
3. 3	7. 5
4. 1	8. 4

EXERCISE 6

1. OK
2. pennies
3. crowns
4. blueberries
5. witches
6. puppies
7. blankets
8. secretaries

EXERCISE 7

1. tomatoes
2. attorneys-at-law
3. bagfuls
4. brothers-in-law
5. OK
6. knives
7. photos
8. leaves
9. OK
10. potatoes
11. OK
12. cupfuls
13. studios
14. senators-elect

EXERCISE 8

1. OK
2. crises
3. sunglasses
4. policemen
5. teeth
6. OK
7. servicewomen
8. deer
9. godchildren
10. criteria

EXERCISE 9

1. cities
2. churches
3. chairwomen
4. crises
5. monkeys
6. brothers-in-law
7. babies
8. teeth
9. beliefs
10. solos
11. checks
12. potatoes
13. wives
14. stories
15. lights
16. replays
17. spoonfuls
18. fish
19. bookshelves
20. grandchildren
21. vacancies
22. crashes
23. annexes
24. quartzes
25. criteria

70

EXERCISE 10

1. OK
2. bus's
3. landlord's
4. miners'
5. weeks'
6. OK
7. protesters'
8. Jones's
9. parents'
10. OK
11. workers'
12. Gross's
13. OK
14. today's
15. Boys'

EXERCISE 11

1. José's
2. David's
3. OK
4. people's
5. OK
6. women's
7. Steve's
8. OK
9. Sally's
10. OK

EXERCISE 12

1. fewer
2. These
3. OK
4. less
5. OK
6. advice
7. many
8. deal

EXERCISE 13

1. 1
2. 1
3. 5
4. 3
5. 1
6. 3
7. 1
8. 1
9. 2
10. 4
11. 1
12. 4
13. 2
14. 5
15. 2
16. 1
17. 3
18. 4
19. 2
20. 1
21. 4
22. 3
23. 4
24. 2
25. 5

EXERCISE 14

1. stirred
2. is
3. reported
4. slips, will break
5. will decide
6. left, was
7. is
8. give
9. dimmed, booed
10. pour, cause
11. saw, hit
12. slams, jumps
13. baked, were
14. spread
15. write
16. am
17. thinks
18. finish, take

EXERCISE 15

1. rained
2. carried
3. OK
4. employed
5. dried
6. OK
7. scrubbed
8. committed

EXERCISE 16

1. threw
2. wrote
3. ran
4. slept
5. struck
6. swam
7. caught
8. flew
9. stole
10. was
11. said
12. lost
13. felt
14. saw
15. taught

EXERCISE 17

1. eaten
2. seen
3. go
4. to write
5. written
6. got
7. felt
8. spoken
9. hurt
10. heard
11. to get
12. broken

13. slept
14. left
15. frozen
16. doing
17. drink
18. swept
19. known
20. think
21. done
22. bought
23. answering
24. went
25. sung
26. ate
27. sat
28. order
29. taking
30. trying

EXERCISE 18

1. have loved
2. took
3. have enjoyed
4. remember
5. boarded
6. carried
7. packed
8. helped
9. gave
10. felt
11. saw
12. looked
13. flashed, were flashing
14. stopped
15. ate
16. am
17. has gone
18. enjoy
19. feel
20. stare
21. forget
22. am planning
23. live, am living
24. to visit
25. will attend, are going to attend
26. will take, is going to take
27. will spend, am going to spend
28. will forget, am going to forget

EXERCISE 19

1. 2	**9.** 1
2. 1	**10.** 1
3. 2	**11.** 4
4. 3	**12.** 2
5. 5	**13.** 5
6. 3	**14.** 2
7. 4	**15.** 2
8. 3	**16.** 3

EXERCISE 20

1. shade
2. need
3. is
4. like
5. drinks
6. have
7. buy
8. were
9. is
10. are
11. have
12. revolves
13. curls
14. charge
15. meet
16. floods
17. are
18. were
19. take
20. have

EXERCISE 21

1. Is
2. don't
3. Does
4. Have
5. wasn't
6. OK
7. doesn't
8. are
9. Have
10. OK
11. Are
12. aren't
13. Do
14. OK
15. Does

EXERCISE 22

1. provide	**5.** costs
2. is	**6.** takes
3. are	**7.** are
4. belong	**8.** is

EXERCISE 23

1. is
2. are
3. grow
4. were
5. are
6. wasn't
7. are
8. is
9. goes
10. were
11. comes
12. come
13. are
14. does
15. are
16. are
17. do
18. sit

EXERCISE 24

1. was
2. was
3. is
4. is
5. has
6. disagree
7. has
8. wasn't
9. Is
10. plays
11. take
12. causes
13. seems
14. has
15. was

EXERCISE 25

1. is
2. uses
3. come
4. helps
5. sign
6. looks
7. are
8. Has

EXERCISE 26

1. grow
2. keep
3. shakes
4. is
5. are
6. is
7. leaves
8. are
9. uses
10. are
11. are
12. was
13. are
14. has
15. have

EXERCISE 27

1. are	**5.** tells
2. is	**6.** has
3. are	**7.** is
4. is	**8.** were

EXERCISE 28

1. opens	**5.** needs
2. burn	**6.** admire
3. own	**7.** sleeps
4. prefers	**8.** include

EXERCISE 29

1.	don't	23.	sell
2.	has	24.	is
3.	visit	25.	are
4.	doesn't	26.	are
5.	was	27.	doesn't
6.	is	28.	Were
7.	cause	29.	are
8.	was	30.	say
9.	were	31.	is
10.	claims	32.	Does
11.	hasn't	33.	wants
12.	doesn't	34.	needs
13.	eats	35.	are
14.	makes	36.	were
15.	need	37.	is
16.	has	38.	is
17.	is	39.	have
18.	grow	40.	are
19.	is	41.	is
20.	sound	42.	is
21.	makes	43.	interviews
22.	adds	44.	lies
		45.	gives

EXERCISE 30

1. us
2. Our
3. your
4. mine
5. her
6. himself
7. yourself
8. me
9. I
10. you
11. themselves
12. ours
13. hers
14. We
15. us
16. him
17. themselves
18. theirs
19. her
20. He
21. him
22. they

EXERCISE 31

1. I
2. We, they
3. they
4. He
5. him
6. them
7. her
8. he
9. They, we
10. me
11. us
12. me

EXERCISE 32

1. Whom
2. Who
3. whom
4. who
5. whom
6. who
7. whom
8. whomever
9. Whoever
10. whoever
11. whomever
12. Whoever

EXERCISE 33

1.	I	7.	we
2.	she	8.	he, she
3.	me	9.	he
4.	he	10.	she
5.	we	11.	him
6.	she	12.	they

EXERCISE 34

1.	Your	11.	We
2.	I	12.	us
3.	my	13.	you
4.	We	14.	We
5.	us	15.	us
6.	my	16.	he
7.	I	17.	Your, me
8.	we	18.	We
9.	your	19.	We
10.	his	20.	myself

EXERCISE 35

1.	their	7.	its
2.	his	8.	their
3.	its	9.	their
4.	its	10.	their
5.	their	11.	their
6.	their	12.	her

EXERCISE 36

1. his or her
2. OK
3. his or her
4. his
5. him or her
6. his or her
7. OK
8. him or her

EXERCISE 37

1.	1	14.	2
2.	2	15.	3
3.	5	16.	5
4.	1	17.	2
5.	3	18.	1
6.	2	19.	1
7.	5	20.	2
8.	3	21.	5
9.	1	22.	3
10.	3	23.	1
11.	3	24.	4
12.	5	25.	4
13.	2		

EXERCISE 38

1. stylish; adverb
2. flowers; adjective
3. blanket; adjective
4. cereal; adjective
5. scraped; adverb
6. peanuts; adjective
7. crept; adverb
8. come; adverb
9. go; adverb
10. movies; adjective
11. finished; adverb
12. water; adjective
13. person; adjective
14. sorry; adverb
15. frightened; adverb

EXERCISE 39

1. positively
2. possibly
3. definitely
4. historically
5. truly
6. finally
7. OK
8. messily
9. strangely
10. sincerely

EXERCISE 40

1. good
2. awful
3. badly
4. sore
5. well
6. noisy
7. well
8. easy
9. beautiful
10. good
11. strong
12. nervous
13. well
14. good
15. well
16. dirty
17. familiar
18. ready
19. healthy
20. short
21. eager
22. alert
23. bravely
24. proud
25. warm
26. sour
27. good
28. angry
29. carefully
30. good

EXERCISE 41

1. hasn't
2. any
3. nothing
4. has
5. isn't
6. has
7. no one
8. have
9. isn't
10. can
11. any
12. ever

EXERCISE 42

1. This
2. a
3. OK
4. these
5. an
6. those

EXERCISE 43

1. smallest
2. harder
3. more beautifully
4. strangest
5. less patient
6. the deepest
7. longer
8. most popular
9. more eager
10. rainiest

EXERCISE 44

1. worse
2. hungriest
3. further
4. hottest
5. most
6. uglier
7. most gently
8. curliest
9. heavier
10. easiest
11. tallest
12. deeper
13. fewer
14. most carefully
15. better
16. latest
17. farther
18. poorest
19. rainier
20. more uneven

EXERCISE 45

1. 1
2. 5
3. 1
4. 1
5. 2
6. 4
7. 3
8. 2
9. 3
10. 2
11. 5
12. 2
13. 1
14. 4
15. 1
16. 4
17. 3
18. 4